BROOKE BOND TEA CARDS REFERENCE BOOK

complied by
IAN A LAKER

ISBN 978-1-906397-02-9

Published November 2007

By

**THE LONDON CIGARETTE CARD COMPANY LIMITED
SUTTON ROAD, SOMERTON, SOMERSET, TA11 6QP
ENGLAND**
Telephone 01458 273452
Fax 01458 273515
Email: cards@londoncigcard.co.uk

Website: www.londoncigcard.co.uk

PREFACE

Arthur Brooke began selling tea from a shop in Manchester in 1869. The business prospered and grew to become Britain's leading tea company. In 1954, when the firm produced their first series of cards, few could have imagined that this was the beginning of a collector's dream, which would endure for almost half a century. With one series following another at regular intervals, Brooke Bond became one of the most prolific and widely respected of all post-war card issuers. The content and quality of production was widely acknowledged as being second to none, and the introduction of albums and wallcharts added to the attraction for collectors of all ages.

Following their success in the U.K., card promotions were extended to the company's overseas operations in Africa and North America. Back home, continuing interest long after the original series disappeared from the packet, led to the 'black-back' reprints being printed to satisfy demand and the company set up its own picture card division to deal with the phenomenal response from collectors.

Towards the end of the 1990s, Brooke Bond perceived, wrongly many would say, that cards as a marketing tool had had their day, and they would concentrate their efforts on other forms of advertising. However, their legacy lives on, and interest in their cards continues unabated.

Although there have been previous reference books on Brooke Bond, it has long been our intention at the London Cigarette Card Company to produce a definitive book providing a complete review of all the tea company's issues. With that in mind, we published in our magazine "Card Collectors News" monthly features collating all the information in our possession. We asked readers to check the details, to tell us about any omissions and to fill in certain gaps in our knowledge. The response was terrific and your input was a great help. So many of you rallied to the cause that I cannot possibly name you all here, but I would like to take this opportunity to express my appreciation for your efforts.

So here it is at last. The Brooke Bond Tea Card Reference Book, which I am certain will make a valuable contribution to the hobby. Equally certain is that as time goes by more information will come to light and I will use the columns of "Card Collectors News" to keep you up-to-date with developments.

Ian A. Laker
November 2007

THE BROOKE BOND STORY

The Tea Company's First Hundred Years   *by John Harrison*

Almost half a century ago, John Harrison researched the firm's history and produced "Brooke Bond – The First 100 Years" which was published in the July 1977 issue of Card Collectors News magazine and is reprinted here for the useful background information it provides.

Brooke Bond was founded by Arthur Brooke, who was born in 1845 at Ashton-Under-Lyne. At the age of 24 he opened his own retail shop at 29 Market Street, Manchester, selling tea, coffee and sugar only for cash over the counter, an innovation in a trade hampered by credit and debts. His teas were always reliable, were packaged in ½lb and 1lb paper bags and he is reputed as being most scrupulous about giving full weight. Arthur Brooke prospered and opened more shops in Liverpool, Leeds and Bradford. In 1872 he moved to London. He took a warehouse in Whitechapel, London using 129 Whitechapel High Street as a company office. By 1887 matters were moving ahead. Seeking new ideas and modern methods he visited America, visiting New Orleans and Chicago (and opened a shop). In 1892 Arthur Brooke took his company to the market. It became Brooke Bond & Company Ltd. The company took over substantial properties with the business becoming primarily wholesale.

Brooke Bond diamond jubilee issue. Note the comma between Brooke and Bond. Actual size of card 84 x 45mm.

In 1907 the company decided to introduce a van delivery system and thus cease to be tied to wholesale agents. Expansion came again with the opening of a new warehouse in Goulston Street, London. In 1910 the company was supplying tea to the Royal Navy under an Admiralty contract and this was soon followed by a contract to the War Office to supply tea for the Army. Then began the years of mechanisation. The tea packets were now being printed by the Berkshire Printing Company at Reading, which was being developed on the foundations of a printworks bought by Arthur Brooke in 1902. From 1911 the tea factories were trying out automatic weighing and packing machines and electric bag-making machines.

THE EYE OF THE CITY.

THE TOWN HALL, MANCHESTER.   Brooke, Bond's Registered Series.

One of "Brooke Bond's Registered Series" of Manchester silhouettes from around 1900. Size 135 x 89mm the subjects are:
The Eye of The City – The Town Hall, Manchester
Religion and Piety – The Cathedral, Manchester
Sick and Suffering – The Infirmary, Manchester
Trade and Commerce – The Royal Exchange, Manchester
Truth and Justice – The Assize Court, Manchester

To maintain distribution at the outbreak of war in 1914 packing could not be concentrated in London. A warehouse block was leased in Trafford Park, Manchester. Gerald Brooke, now the chairman after Arthur's retirement in 1910, hastily recruited staff, including forty married women and he and his manager personally handled tea chests from the siding to the factory.

As the war ended returning servicemen were absorbed into the expanding business. Some did not return. One was John Travers Cornwell, a former Brooke Bond van boy who met death and fame as a sixteen-year old boy 1st class in the Royal Navy. At the battle of Jutland he stayed at his gun turret in H.M.S. Chester as his companions died around him, until eventually he too was killed. Posthumously he was awarded the Victoria Cross – a fact recorded on many series of cigarette cards.

In 1922 a new blending and packing factory was opened in Trafford Park. With its automatic machines it was then the most up-to-date tea factory in the world. Brooke Bond (India) Limited was founded in 1912. From 1925 the Indian company started its own branches in Egypt and East Africa. Working conditions – almost unprecedented at that time in India in 1926 – were introduced, maximum pay, paid holidays, daily inspection by an Indian doctor, canteen meals and a laundry.

Back home in the U.K the van delivery system was making the name of Brooke Bond familiar in every street in Britain, giving visible evidence that once or twice a week fresh packet teas were being delivered to countless small grocers and the corner shops. Until the late 'Twenties, most of the vans were horse-drawn. The early Trojan motor vans had solid tyres. By the 1930s the "little red vans" were calling on 190,000 shops in Britain and the van system expanded to 850 vans.

In 1935 a new blend called 'Dividend' was introduced in order to fight increasing competition, mainly from the Co-operative Wholesale Society – the giant of the British tea trade in those days. Today 'Dividend' tea remains one of the most popular blends that graces the nation's teapots. Another blend was launched in the 1930s. It was named 'Pre-gest-Tea'. In those days tea was sometimes sold on its medicinal properties to aid digestion. Legal objections were made against the use of the word 'digestive' in association with tea. Thus 'Pre-gest-Tea' became known to the trade as 'PG Tips', as it still is to millions of shoppers.

In 1939, London headquarters were dispersed from the East End of London. Seven new factories were opened in areas away from the possible bombing. Despite wartime problems, loss of manpower, hazards of distribution, petrol rationing and limitations imposed by tea control, Brooke Bond supplied the cups that cheered the beleaguered nation. With the end of tea rationing in 1952 a new era commenced in the tea trade. Gerald Brooke retired after forty years' service and handed over the chairmanship to his son John. In 1956 the Suez operation took British and French troops into the Canal Zone. The company's factory became the temporary HQ of the British Airborne Division.

The years passed and Brooke Bond became an international name having their companies, estates and factories all over the world – in USA, Canada, East Africa, India and Ceylon, with partnership in Bushell's of Australia. Diversification came in printing, engineering, brokerage, insurance, cheese manufacturing and merchandising in spices and other channels. Later, a wave of expansion and modernisation led to the merger of Brooke Bond with Liebig's Extract Meat Company in May 1968.

One of the many successful advertising promotions was the launching of the first picture cards on the 16th August 1954; a series of 20 cards depicting natural history and called *British Birds*, by the late Frances Pitt. Next a series of 50 cards *Wild Flowers* by John Markham F.R.P.S. was introduced on 28th March 1955. When *British Birds* were withdrawn the company was inundated with postal requests for odd cards, albums and sets from the series and the company decided to set up a special section to deal with the flood of enquiries. (The Picture Card Division today handles over one million postal requests annually). Since 1954 Brooke Bond has introduced thirty different series of cards and albums at home, and selections of sets and albums in many overseas countries.

With the inauguration of independent television in 1955 Brooke Bond became one of the first companies to exploit the advertising possibilities of the new medium. Soon the Brooke Bond chimps were in demand for public appearances, and they also appeared at the Saturday morning film shows and circus treats for young children. The company's mobile film units presented film shows to members of women's and other institutions all over Britain.

In July 1969 Brooke Bond Tea Limited and Oxo Limited joined together to form a new company called Brooke Bond Oxo Limited, the UK trading subsidiary of Brooke Bond Liebig Limited.

BROOKE BOND TEA CARD ISSUES

Series listed in date of issue order

ISSUES OF GREAT BRITAIN
Single card sets

B1	20	British Birds by Frances Pitt	1954
B2	50	Wild Flowers Series 1	1955
B3	50	Out Into Space	1956
B4	50	Bird Portraits	1957
B5	50	British Wild Life	1958
B6	50	Wild Flowers Series 2	1959
B7	50	Freshwater Fish	1960
B8	50	African Wild Life	1961
B9	50	Tropical Birds	1961
B10	50	Asian Wild Life	1962
B11	50	British Butterflies	1963
B12	50	Wildlife in Danger	1963
B13	50	Wild Flowers Series 3	1964
B14	50	Butterflies of the World	1964
B15	50	Wild Birds in Britain	1965
B16	50	Transport Through The Ages	1966
B17	50	Trees in Britain	1966
B18	50	Flags and Emblems of the World	1967
B19	50	British Costume	1967
B20	50	History of the Motor Car	1968
B21	50	Famous People	1969
B22	50	The Saga of Ships	1970
B23	50	The Race Into Space	1971
B24	50	Prehistoric Animals	1972
B25	50	History of Aviation	1972
B26	50	Adventurers and Explorers	1973
B27	50	The Sea - Our Other World	1974
B28	50	Inventors and Inventions	1975
B29	50	Wonders of Wildlife	1976
B30	40	Play Better Soccer	1976
B31	40	Police File	1977
B32	40	Vanishing Wildlife	1978
B33	40	Olympic Greats	1979
B34	40	Woodland Wildlife	1980
B35	40	Small Wonders	1981
B36	50	Queen Elizabeth I – Queen Elizabeth II	1983
B37	50	Features of the World	1984
B38	40	Incredible Creatures	1985
B39	12	30 Years of the Chimps 1956 - 1986	1986
B40	40	Unexplained Mysteries of the World	1987
B41	12	The Language of Tea	1988
B42	50	Discovering Our Coast	1989

B43	25	The Magical World of Disney	1989
B44	25	A Journey Downstream	1990
B45	12	Teenage Mutant HeroTurtles - Dimension Xescapade	1991
B46	40	Olympic Challenge 1992	1992
B47	40	Natural Neighbours	1992
B48	20	The Dinosaur Trail with Kevin Tipps	1993
B49	24	Creatures of Legend with Kevin Tipps	1994
B50	40	Going Wild – Wildlife Survival Challenge	1994
B51	50	The Secret Diary of Kevin Tipps	1995
B52	40	40 Years of the Chimps Television Advertising	1995
B53	45	The Magical, Mystical World of Pyramids	1996
B54	30	The Wonderful World of Kevin Tipps	1997
B55	20	International Soccer Stars	1998

Double card sets

B36	25	Queen Elizabeth I – Queen Elizabeth II	1983
B37	25	Features of the World	1984
B38	20	Incredible Creatures	1985
B40	20	Unexplained Mysteries of the World	1987
B42	25	Discovering Our Coast	1989
B43	25	The Magical World of Disney	1989
B44	25	A Journey Downstream	1990
B45	6	Teenage Mutant HeroTurtles - Dimension Xescapade	1991
B46	20	Olympic Challenge1992	1992
B47	20	Natural Neighbours	1992
B48	10	The Dinosaur Trail with Kevin Tipps	1993
B49	12	Creatures of Legend with Kevin Tipps	1994
B50	20	Going Wild – Wildlife Survival Challenge	1994

Reprint card series

B6	50	Wild Flowers Series 2	1973
B7	50	Freshwater Fish	1973
B8	50	African Wild Life	1973
B9	50	Tropical Birds	1974
B11	50	British Butterflies	1973
B12	50	Wildlife in Danger	1973
B15	50	Wild Birds in Britain	1973
B16	50	Transport Through The Ages	1973
B17	50	Trees in Britain	1973
B18	50	Flags and Emblems of the World	1973
B19	50	British Costume	1973
B21	50	Famous People	1973
B22	50	The Saga of Ships	1973
B20	50	History of the Motor Car	1974
B23	50	The Race Into Space	1974
B32	40	Vanishing Wildlife	1988
B33	40	Olympic Greats	1988
B34	40	Woodland Wildlife	1988
B35	40	Small Wonders	1988
B36	50	Queen Elizabeth I – Queen Elizabeth II	1988
B42	50	Discovering Our Coast	1989
B53	45	The Magical, Mystical World of Pyramids	1998

Miscellaneous Issues
-	1	1966 World Cup Souvenir - Booklet	1966
-	15	Place the Face Bingo Cards.	1972
-	10	Polyfilla Modelling Cards	1974
-	50	Zena Skinner International Cookery	1974
-	22	Tea Quiz Competition.	1986
-	48	40 Years of Cards (1954 – 1994).	1994
-	19	Tea Leaf Oracle.	1999

Playing Cards
-	48	Snip Snap – The Decimal Currency Game.	1970
-	36	British Costume – Family Card Game	1975
-	36	Flags and Emblems – Snap.	1975
-	36	Motor History – Snap.	1975
-	55	P G Tips Get Out!	1995
-	54	P G Tips Playing Cards.	1995
-	36	P G Tips Snap!	1995
-	55	P G Tips Trick Cards.	1995

Advertisement Cards and Inserts
-	1	Why is Crown Cup "Medium Roasted"?	1963
-	1	3 Crown Cups and Saucers	1963
-	2	Danish designed Tableware	1964
-	2	Radio London	1965
-	2	6-Picece Cutlery	1966
-	1	Free Opal Glass Jar	1967
-	1	Play Better Soccer set and album offer	1976
-	1	Play Better Soccer Great New Series!	1976
-	1	Police File New Picture Card Series	1977
-	1	Token – Keep This Token Brooke Bond D	1994
-	1	Token Brooke Bond D 1	1994
-	1	The Tips Family Transfer Kit	1994
-	1	Carefully Decaffeinated.	1994
-	1	Brooke Bond Orange Label.	1994
-	1	Brooke Bond D Refreshing Tea	1994
-	1	PG Tips Tipps Family 1997 Calendar	1996
-	1	PG Tips need Your Help!	1999
-	1	Thank You!	1999
-	3	Farewell to Picture Cards	1999
-	1	PG Tips Bean Chimp Offer	2001
-	1	Scratch Card. Are you a PG Tips 2 Go Winner	2005

ISSUES OF IRELAND

B38	48	Incredible Creatures	1986

Miscellaneous Issues
-	7	Catch A Spy	1977

Advertisement Cards and Inserts
-	1	P G Tips Token How to obtain free pens	c1975

ISSUES OF CANADA

CU1	48	Songbirds of North America	1959
CU2	48	Animals of North America.	1960
CU3	48	Wild Flowers of North America	1961
CU4	48	Birds of North America	1962
CU5	48	Dinosaurs	1963
CU6	48	Tropical Birds	1964
CU7	48	African Animals	1964
CU8	48	Butterflies of North America	1965
CU9	48	Candian/American Songbirds	1966
CU10	48	Transportation Through the Ages	1967
CU11	48	Trees of North America	1968
CU12	48	The Space Age	1969
CU13	48	North American Wildlife in Danger	1970
CU14	48	Exploring the Ocean	1971
CU15	48	Animals and Their Young	1972
CU16	48	The Arctic	1973
CU17	48	Indians of Canada	1974

ISSUES OF U S A

CU2	48	Animals of North America	1960
CU3	48	Wild Flowers of North America	1961
CU4	48	Birds of North America	1962
CU5	48	Dinosaurs	1963
CU6	48	Tropical Birds	1964
CU8	48	Butterflies of North America	1965
CU9	48	Candian/American Songbirds	1966

ISSUES OF SOUTHERN RHODESIA & EAST AFRICA

SR1	50	Bird Portraits	1960
SR2	50	African Wild Life	1961
SR3	50	Tropical Birds	1962
SR4	50	Asian Wild Life	1963
SR5	50	Wildlife in Danger	1964
SR6	50	African Birds	1965
SR7	50	Butterflies of the World	1966

ISSUES OF SOUTH AFRICA

SA1	50	African Wild Life/Wild Van Afrika	1965
SA2	50	African Wild Life/Wild Van Afrika	1965
SA3	50	Out Into Space	1966
SA4	50	Our Pets	1967

ISSUES OF MUSGRAVE-BROOKE BOND IRELAND

MBB1	20	British Birds by Frances Pitt	1964
MBB2	50	British Wild Life	1964
MBB3	50	Butterflies of the World	1965
MBB4	50	Transport Through The Ages	1966

Miscellaneous Issues

- 39 Matchmaker Gift Cards   1967

ISSUES OF BROOKE BOND LIEBIG ITALY

-	6	Serie 323 La Nativita (The Nativity)	1971
-	6	Serie 324 Storia Della Macchina Per Scrivere	
		(History of the Typewriter)	1972
-	6	Serie 325 La Resurrezione (The Resurrection)	1972
-	6	Serie 327 Le Grandin Sfide (Historical Fights)	1972
-	6	Serie 328 Autoritratti Di Grandi Pittori Italiani	
		(Self- Portraits of Famous Artists)	1972
-	6	Serie 329 Cosi' Vedono Gli Animali (How Animals See) 1st series	1973
-	6	Serie 330 Ludwig Van Beethoven	1973
-	6	Serie 331 Cacciatori Di Microbi (The Fight Against Microbes)	
		1st series	1973
-	6	Serie 332 Cosi' Vedono Gli Animali (How Animals See) 2nd series	1973
-	6	Serie 333 Storia Del Circo (The Story of the Circus) 1st series	1973
-	6	Serie 334 Cacciatori Di Microbi (The Fight Against Microbes)	
		2nd series	1973
-	6	Serie 335 Storia Del Circo (The Story of the Circus) 2nd series	1973
-	6	Serie 336 Marina Da Guerra (War at Sea)	1973
-	6	Serie 337 Il Regno Animale (Animals)	1973
-	6	Gli Uccelli Protetti (Protected Birds) No series number	1975
-	6	Serie 298 Uniformologia Antica (Old Military Dress) 1st series	1975
-	6	Serie 299 Uniformologia Antica (Old military Dress) 2nd series	1975
-	6	Serie 320 Come Siamo Andati Sulla Luna (Journey to the Moon)	
		1st series	1975
-	6	Serie 326 Come Siamo Andati Sulla Luna (Journey to the Moon)	
		2nd series	1975

BROOKE BOND TEA CARD ISSUES

Series listed in alpabetical order

ISSUES OF GREAT BRITAIN

Adventurers and Explorers. Size 69 x 37mm coloured numbered series of 50 issued in 1973 backs printed in black. Wallchart issued.
Two printings of card number 33
    A) With the word "to" in penultimate line of text
    B) Without word "to" in penultimate line of text
Special album issued
    1) With insert order form stapled in centre fold. Form printed over two pages front in green.
    2) Non insert order form without staple marks in centre fold. Form printed over two pages in green obtained direct from Brooke Bond. Number rubber stamped on back.

African Wild Life. Size 69 x 37mm coloured numbered series of 50
There are two printings of this set
    A) Back printed in blue original issue issued in 1961
    B) Back printed in black reprint issue issued in 1973
Special album issued with four printings
  A) Original – Matt cover with price. Small print on front in black
  B) Original - Matt cover with price. Small print on front in bluish grey
    1) Insert order form tag on left folded upwards. Printed in blue
    2) Insert order form tag on left folded downwards. Printed in blue
    3) Non insert order form with no tag obtained direct from Brooke Bond. Printed in blue
  C) Reprint – Glossy cover with price
  D) Reprint – Glossy cover without price
Note: Southern Rhodesia & East Africa album front cover without price, but red line under "C. F. Tunnicliffe, R. A.", back cover also differs from Great Britain issue with no text underneath Brooke Bond in oval. Wallchart issued titled East African Wildlife.

Asian Wild Life. Size 69 x 37mm coloured numbered series of 50 issued in 1962 backs printed in blue. Wallchart issued.
Special album issued
  1) Insert order form tag on left hand side. Printed in black
  2) Insert order form tag on right hand side. Printed in black

Bird Portraits. Size 69 x 37mm coloured numbered series of 50 issued in 1957 backs printed in blue. Wallchart issued.
There are two printings of this set
    A) Without address (1st printing)
    B) With address (2nd printing)
Special album issued with two printings (no insert order form).
    A) Solid border to outline of card space
    B) Dotted border to outline of card space
Note: there were 4 booklets issued in connection with this set titled Brooke Bond Cut-out Series Bird Portraits. Coloured, size 156 x 124mm, 12 pages in each
    1. Goldfinch   3. Sheld Duck
    2. Lapwing   4. Song Thrush

British Birds by Frances Pitt. Size 69 x 37mm coloured numbered series of 20 issued in 1954 backs printed in blue. Special album issued cover price 3d. (no insert order form).
There are two printings of this set
    A) Printed on white card
    B) Printed on cream card
Note: Musgrave-Brooke Bond album, cover with price 6d. (See Issues of Musgrave-Brooke Bond Ireland)

British Butterflies. Size 69 x 37mm coloured numbered series of 50. Wallchart issued.
There are two printings of this set
    A) Backs printed in blue original issue issued in 1963
    B) Backs printed in black reprint issue issued in 1973
Special album issued with three printings
    A) Original – Matt cover with price
        1) Insert order form tag on left hand side. Printed in black
        2) Insert order form tag on right hand side. Printed in black
    B) Reprint – Glossy cover with price
    C) Reprint – Glossy cover without price

British Costume. Size 69 x 37mm coloured numbered series of 50.
There are two printings of this set
    A) Backs printed in blue original issue issued in 1967
    B) Backs printed in black reprint issue issued in 1973
There are two printings of numbers 3, 4, 23, 24. in the blue back issue
    No 3 A) Both figures in yellow (correct card)
            B) Right hand figure in red and white (front of card number 4)
    No 4 A) Right hand figure in red and white (correct card)
            B) Both figures in yellow (front of card number 3)
    No 23 A) Mauve background pink dress (correct card)
            B) Red background red and silver dress (front of card number 24)
    No 24 A) Red background red and silver dress (correct card)
            B) Mauve background pink dress (front of card number 23)
Special album issued with three printings
    A) Original – Cover with price with printers credit "Berkshire Printing" inside back cover
        1) Insert order form tag on left hand side. Printed in black
        2) Insert order form tag on right hand side. Printed in black
        3) Non insert order form with no tag obtained direct from Brooke Bond. Printed in black. Number rubber stamped on back.
    B) Reprint – Cover with price without printers credit "Berkshire Printing" inside back cover
    C) Reprint – Cover without price with printers credit "Berkshire Printing" inside back cover
Wallchart issued in two sizes
    A) 990 x 838 mm
    B) 762 x 508 mm

British Wild Life. Size 69 x 37mm coloured numbered series of 50 issued in 1958 backs printed in blue. Special album issued (no insert order form). Wallchart issued.
There are three printings of this set.
    A) Brooke Bond & Co Ltd (first printing)
    B) Brooke Bond (Great Britain) Ltd (second printing)
    C) Brooke Bond Tea Ltd (third printing)
Note: Musgrave-Brooke Bond album issued with Musgrave Brothers Ltd on back. (See Issues of Musgrave-Brooke Bond Ireland)
Part of this set was also issued by the R S P C A. as follows
    A) Anonymous issue numbered series of 16 back inscribed "This picture is published by courtesy of Brooke Bond Tea Ltd." Number 1 is Shetland Pony.
    B) Inscribed R S P C A. Numbered series of 16 back inscribed "This picture is published by courtesy of…" Number 1 is Welsh Mountain Pony. There are two printings
        1) Back with Brooke Bond Tea Ltd.
        2) Back with Brooke Bond Oxo Ltd.

Butterflies of the World. Size 69 x 37mm coloured numbered series of 50 issued in 1964 backs printed in blue. Wallchart issued.
Special album issued. Cover with price 6d.
    1) Insert order form tag on left hand side. Printed in black
    2) Insert order form tag on right hand side. Printed in black
Note: Southern Rhodesia album, cover with price 9d. (See Issues of Southern Rhodesia & East Africa)

Creatures of Legend with Kevin Tipps. Coloured numbered issued in 1994 backs printed in black and red. Wallchart issued.
There are two printings of this set.
    A) Set of 24 size 78 x 47mm one picture per card.
    B) Set of 12 size 78 x 94 mm two pictures per card numbered consecutively 1-2, 3-4, etc.
Special album issued with insert order form
    1) Insert order form valid until 31.12.94 stapled in centre fold. Form printed in blue with Special Limited Edition 40 Years of Cards offer on right hand side.
    2) Non insert order form valid until 31.12.94 without staple marks in centre fold. Form printed in blue with Special Limited Edition 40 Years of Cards offer on right hand side, obtained direct from Brooke Bond

The Dinosaur Trail with Kevin Tipps. Coloured numbered issued in 1993 backs printed in green and red. Wallchart issued.
There are four printings of this set.
    A) Set of 20 size 69 x 37mm one picture per card
        1) Postcode BB1 1PG (first printing)
        2) Postcode BB11 1PG (second printing)
    B) Set of 10 size 69 x 74mm two pictures per card numbered consecutively 1-2, 3-4, etc.
        1) Postcode BB1 1PG (first printing)
        2) Postcode BB11 1PG (second printing)
Special album issued with two printings

The Dinosaur Trail with Kevin Tipps Continued
    A) Back outside cover with "© Marshall...."
    A) Back outside cover without "© Marshall...."
        Insert order form valid until 31.3.94 stapled in centre fold printed in black with PG Tips Picture Cards Questionnaire on left hand side.
Note: This set was also issued with The Daily Mirror and World of Dinosaurs magazine
The Daily Mirror issue printed on 8 sheets with 6 cards printed on each sheet with advert for the album, cards, wallchart and models. Size 205 x152mm (Postcode BB1 1PG) as follows:
    A) Numbers 1, 2, 3, 15, 16, 17
    B) Numbers 1, 2, 3, 18, 19, 20
    C) Numbers 4, 5, 6, 12, 13, 14
    D) Numbers 4, 5, 6, 15, 16, 17
    E) Numbers 7, 8, 9, 12, 13, 14
    F) Numbers 7, 8, 9, 15, 16, 17
    G) Numbers 10, 11, 12, 1, 2, 3
    H) Numbers 18, 19, 20, 10, 11, 12
The World of Dinosaurs magazine issue printed on 5 sheets with 4 cards printed on each sheet with advert for Dinosaur models, adventure game etc. Size 290 x 205mm (Postcode BB1 1PG) as follows
    A) Numbers 1,2,3,4
    B) Numbers 5,6,7,8
    C) Numbers 9,10,11,12
    D) Numbers 13,14,15,16
    E) Numbers 17,18,19,20 (Note this sheet is believed not to have been issued)

Discovering Our Coast. Coloured numbered. Special album issued. Wallchart issued.
There are three printings of this set
    A) Set of 50 size 69 x 37mm one picture per card
        1) Backs printed in blue original issue issued in 1989
        2) Backs printed in black reprint issue issued in 1992
    B) Set of 25 size 69 x 74mm two pictures per card numbered consecutively 1-2, 3-4,etc
There are two printings of numbers 2, 8, 31 in both blue back printings
    No 2 A) Text third line "The National Trust"
            B) Text third line "National Trust for Scotland"
    No 8 A) Text third line "north-west"
            B) Text third line "north-east"
    No 31 A) Text in two paragraphs
            B) Text in three paragraphs
Same error also appears in double card printing
Special album issued with insert order form loose not stapled form printed in blue valid until 31.8.89. Album issued with Amateur Art & Photography Competition insert stapled in centre with closing date 31st March 1989.
Note: There is no visible difference between original and the reprinted album.

Famous People. Size 69 x 37mm coloured numbered series of 50. Wallchart issued
There are two printings of this set
    A) Backs printed in blue original issue issued in 1969
    B) Backs printed in black reprint issue issued in 1973
Special album issued with four printings

A) Original – Cover with price with printers credit "Berkshire Printing" inside back cover plus
  1) Insert order form stapled in centre fold. Form printed in red. Famous People pictures offer on left hand side printed in colour.
  2) Non insert order form. Form printed in red obtained direct from Brooke Bond. Number rubber stamped on back. Order form only, no Famous People offer attached to left hand side.
B) Reprint – Cover with price without printers credit "Berkshire Printing" inside back cover
C) Reprint – Cover without price with printers credit "Berkshire Printing" inside back cover
D) Reprint – Cover without price without printers credit "Berkshire Printing" inside back cover

Note: There was a trial printing of this set which was laminated both sides but was never issued in the packets.

Features of the World. Coloured numbered issued in 1984 backs printed in green. Special album issued with insert order form
There are two printings of this set
  A) Set of 50 size 69 x 37mm one picture per card.
  B) Set of 25 size 69 x 74mm two pictures per card numbered 1-5, 2-6, 3-7, 4-8 ,9-13, 10-14, 11-15, 12-16, 17-21, 18-22, 19-23, 20-24, 25-50, 26-30, 27-31, 28-32, 29-33, 34-38, 35-39, 36-40, 37-41, 42-46, 43-47, 44-48, 45-49.
Special album issued
  1) Insert order form valid until 31.12.84 stapled in centre fold printed on two pages. Form printed in red
  2) Non insert order form valid until 31.12.84 without staple marks in centre fold. Form printed in red obtained direct from Brooke Bond.
Separate insert titled "Features of the World Quiz Answer Sheet" issued with the album.

Flags and Emblems of the World. Size 69 x 37mm coloured numbered series of 50. Wallchart issued.
There are two printings of this set
  A) Backs printed in blue original issue issued in 1967
  B) Backs printed in black reprint issue issued in 1973
Special album issued with two printings
  A) Original – Matt cover with printers credit "Berkshire Printing" on last page
    1) Insert order form tag on left hand side. Printed in green
    2) Insert order form tag on right hand side. Printed in green
    3) Non insert order form with no tag obtained direct from Brooke Bond. Printed in green. Number rubber stamped on back.
  B) Reprint – Glossy cover without printers credit "Berkshire Printing" on last page

40 Years of the Chimps Television Advertising. Size 89 x 63mm coloured numbered series of 40 issued in 1995 backs printed in black and green.
Special album issued with two printings.
  A) With "17 Roadworks" printed in red at the bottom left hand corner on page for number 26
  B) Without "17 Roadworks" printed in red at the bottom left hand corner on page for number 26
Insert order form loose not stapled. Form printed in black valid until 31.3.97

Freshwater Fish. Size 69 x 37mm, coloured numbered series of 50. Wallchart issued.
There are two printings of this set
    A) Backs printed in blue original issue, issued in 1960
    B) Backs printed in black reprint issue, issued in 1973
Special album issued with three printings
    A) Original – Matt cover with price
        Insert order form tag on left folded upwards. Printed in black
    B) Reprint – Glossy cover with price
    C) Reprint – Glossy cover without price

Going Wild – Wildlife Survival Challenge. Coloured numbered issued in 1994, backs printed in black and green. Wallchart issued
There are two printings of this set.
    A) Set of 40 size 78 x 47mm one picture per card.
    B) Set of 20 size 78 x 94 mm two pictures per card numbered consecutively 1-2, 3-4, etc.
Note: This set was also issued with The Sunday Mirror printed on 8 sheets with 6 cards printed on each sheet size 234 x169mm, as follows:
    A) Numbers 1, 2, 3, 4, 6, 7
    B) Numbers 5, 8, 9, 10, 11, 12
    C) Numbers 5, 13, 19, 24, 25, 31
    D) Numbers 8, 18, 37, 38, 39, 40
    E) Numbers 13, 14, 15, 16, 17, 18
    F) Numbers 19, 20, 21, 22, 23, 24
    G) Numbers 25, 26, 27, 28, 29, 30
    H) Numbers 31, 32, 33, 34, 35, 36
Special album issued with insert order form
    1) Insert order form valid until 31.3.95 stapled in centre fold. Form printed in green with Special Limited Edition 40 Years of Cards offer on right hand side.
    2) Non insert order form valid until 31.3.95 without staple marks in centre fold. Form printed in green with Special Limited Edition 40 Years of Cards offer on right hand side, obtained direct from Brooke Bond.
Separate insert stapled in centre fold for Offers from WWF closing date 31 January 1995 issued with the album.

History of Aviation. Size 69 x 37mm coloured numbered series of 50 issued in 1972, backs printed in black.
Special album issued with two printings with insert order form.
    A) Original – Matt inside cover
        1) Insert order form stapled in centre fold with Aircraft Kits offer on left hand side. Form printed in red
        2) Non insert order form without staple marks and Aircraft Kits offer. Form printed in red obtained direct from Brooke Bond. Number rubber stamped on back.
    B) Reprint – Glossy inside cover
Wallchart issued in two sizes
    A) 990 x 838 mm
    B) 762 x 508 mm

History of the Motor Car. Size 69 x 37mm, coloured numbered series of 50.
There are two printings of this set
    A) Back printed in blue original issue, issued in 1968
    B) Back printed in black reprint issue, issued in 1974

Special album issued with three printings
- A) Original – Matt cover with price with insert order form
    1) Insert order form with "Erratum" note below the single cards required section. Printed in red. Half price table lamp offer on left hand side printed in colour
    2) Non insert order form without "Erratum" note below the single cards required section. Printed in red obtained direct from Brooke Bond. Number rubber stamped on back. Order form only, no half price table lamp offer attached to left hand side.
- B) Reprint – Glossy cover with price
- C) Reprint – Glossy cover without price

Wallchart issued in two sizes
- A) 990 x 838 mm
- B) 762 x 508 mm

Incredible Creatures. Coloured numbered series of 40, backs printed in brown
There are seven printings of this set
- A) Set of 40 size 69 x 37mm one picture per card
    1) Address Sheen Lane issued in 1985 (first printing)
    2) Address Walton on Thames inscribed "Picture Card Dept" issued in 1986 (second printing)
    3) Address Walton on Thames inscribed "Dept IC" issued in 1986 (third printing)
    4) Address Walton on Thames inscribed "Dept IC" Thick card with a peel off back revealing a sticky surface issued in 1986 (fourth printing)
- B) Set of 20 size 69 x 74mm two pictures per card numbered consecutively 1-2, 3-4, etc
    1) Address Sheen Lane issued in 1985 (first printing)
    2) Address Walton on Thames inscribed "Picture Card Dept" issued in 1986 (second printing)
    3) Address Walton on Thames inscribed "Dept IC" issued in 1986 (third printing)

Set of 4 Wallcharts issued.(No special album issued)
1) Under the Ground   Numbers 1 to 10
2) In the Sea   Numbers 11 to 20
3) On the Land   Numbers 21 to 30
4) In the Air   Numbers 31 to 40

Note: Set printed with green backs: see Issues of Ireland.

International Soccer Stars. Size 89 x 63mm, coloured numbered series of 20 issued in 1998, backs printed in green. Wallchart issued.
Two printings of card number 5
- A) Player wearing red shorts
- B) Player wearing white shorts

Special album issued (no insert order form) but separate insert stapled in centre fold for Tipps Family vans, books, Robert Harrop figures.
1) Non insert order form valid until 30.4.99. Form printed in black obtained direct from Brooke Bond
2) Non insert order form valid until 31.8.99. Form printed in black obtained direct from Brooke Bond

Note: Leaflet issued re error card number 5 "Dear PG Drinker, We scored an 'own goal', when we first produced our new International Soccer Stars Picture Card series……." Size 210 x 99mm.

Inventors and Inventions. Size 69 x 37mm, coloured numbered series of 50 issued in 1975, backs printed in black. Wallchart issued.
Special album issued
    1) Insert order form stapled in centre fold printed on two pages. Form printed in red
    2) Non insert order form without staple marks in centre fold. Form printed in red obtained direct from Brooke Bond. Number rubber stamped on back.

A Journey Downstream. Coloured numbered issued in 1990 backs printed in blue
There are two printings of this set
    A) Set of 25 size 69 x 37mm one picture per card.
    B) Set of 25 size 69 x 74mm two pictures per card numbered 1-2, 2-3, 3-4, 4-5, to 23-24, 24-25, then 1-25. Therefore containing two complete sets of each picture in the set.
Special album issued
    Insert order form valid until 28.2.91 stapled in centre fold. Form printed in black with "Help Save British Wildlife" on right hand side.

The Language of Tea. Size 69 x 37mm coloured numbered series of 12 issued in 1988 backs printed in green. Thick card with a peel off back revealing a sticky surface. Wallchart issued, no special album issued. Non insert order form printed in green obtained direct from Brooke Bond.

The Magical, Mystical World of Pyramids. Size 89 x 63mm coloured numbered series of 45.
There are two printings of this set
    A) Backs printed in black and red issued in 1996 (first printing)
    B) Backs printed in black only issued in 1998 (second printing)
Special album issued
    1) Insert order form loose not stapled. Form printed in black valid until 31.3.97
    2) Non insert order form loose not stapled. Form printed in black valid until 31.5.97 obtained direct from Brooke Bond

The Magical World of Disney. Coloured numbered issued in 1989 backs printed in black
There are two printings of this set
    A) Set of 25 size 69 x 37mm one picture per card.
    B) Set of 25 size 69 x 74mm two pictures per card numbered 1-2, 2-3, 3-4, 4-5, to 23-24, 24-25, then 1-25. Therefore containing two complete sets of each picture in the set.
Special album issued
    1) Insert order form valid until 31.5.90 stapled in centre fold printed on two pages. Form printed in red
    2) Non insert order form valid until 31.5.90 without staple marks in centre fold printed on two pages. Form printed in red obtained direct from Brooke Bond

Natural Neighbours. Coloured numbered issued in 1992 backs printed in brown. Wallchart issued.
There are two printings of this set
    A) Set of 40 size 69 x 37mm one picture per card
    B) Set of 20 size 69 x 74mm two pictures per card numbered consecutively 1-2, 3-4, etc
Two printings of card number 37
    A) Text in seventh line "for"
    B) Text in seventh line "for for"
Same error also appears in double card printing

Special album issued
  1) Insert order form valid until 30.6.93 stapled in centre fold printed on two pages. Form printed in black with Go Wild Hotline on right hand side
  2) Non insert order form valid until 30.6.93 without staple marks in centre fold printed on two pages. Form printed in black with Go Wild Hotline on right hand side obtained direct from Brooke Bond

Olympic Challenge 1992. Coloured numbered issued in 1992 backs printed in blue. Wallchart issued.
There are two printings of this set
  A) Set of 40 size 69 x 37mm one picture per card
  B) Set of 20 size 69 x 74mm two pictures per card numbered consecutively 1-2, 3-4, etc
Special album issued
  1) Insert order form valid until 31.12.92 stapled in centre fold printed on two pages. Form printed in orange
  2) Non insert order form valid until 31.12.92 without staple marks in centre fold printed on two pages. Form printed in orange obtained direct from Brooke Bond

Olympic Greats. Size 69 x 37mm coloured numbered series of 40. Wallchart issued.
There are two printings of this set
  A) Back printed in green original issue issued in 1979
  B) Back printed in black reprint issue issued in 1988
Special album issued
  1) Insert order form valid until 30.9.80 stapled in centre fold printed on two pages. Form printed in green
  2) Non insert order form valid until 30.9.80 without staple marks in centre fold printed on two pages. Form printed in green but plain back obtained direct from Brooke Bond

Out Into Space. Size 69 x 37mm coloured numbered series of 50 backs printed in blue
There are two printings of this set
  A) Back "Issued with Brooke Bond…" issued in 1956
  B) Back "Issued in packets of Brooke Bond…" issued in 1958
Two printings of number 11 of "Issued in packets of Brooke Bond …" printing only
  A) With words "Inner Planets" and "Outer Planets" on front
  B) Without words "Inner Planets" and "Outer Planets" on front
Special album issued with two printings (no insert order form).
  A) Back cover without words "P G Tips" issued in 1956
  B) Back cover with words "P G Tips" issued in 1958

Play Better Soccer. Size 69 x 37mm coloured numbered series of 40 issued in 1976 backs printed in black
Special album issued with two printings
  A) Inside pages white paper
  B) Inside pages cream paper
    1) Insert order form stapled in centre fold printed on two pages. Form printed in purple
    2) Non insert order form without staple marks in centre fold. Form printed in purple obtained direct from Brooke Bond. Number rubber stamped on back.

Police File. Size 69 x 37mm coloured numbered series of 40 issued in 1977 backs printed in black
Special album issued
    1) Insert order form valid until 31.3.78 stapled in centre fold printed on two pages. Form printed in green
    2) Non insert order form without staple marks in centre fold. Form printed in green with valid date altered by hand to 31.8.78 and Flags & Emblems Snap game crossed out by hand obtained direct from Brooke Bond.

Prehistoric Animals. Size 69 x 37mm coloured numbered series of 50 issued in 1972 backs printed in black. Wallchart issued.
Special album issued
    1) Insert order form stapled in centre fold with British Wild Life Maps offer on left hand side form printed in blue
    2) Non insert order form without staple marks and Maps offer. Form printed in blue obtained direct from Brooke Bond. Number rubber stamped on back.

Queen Elizabeth I – Queen Elizabeth II. Coloured numbered. Wallchart issued.
There are three printings of this set
    A) Set of 50 size 69 x 37mm one picture per card
        1) Back printed in blue original issue issued in 1983
        2) Back printed in black reprint issue issued in 1988
    B) Set of 25 size 69 x 74mm two pictures per card numbered 1-5, 2-6, 3-7, 4-8, 9-13, 10-14, 11-15, 12-16, 17-21, 18-22, 19-23, 20-24, 26-30, 27-31, 28-32, 29-33, 34-38, 35-39, 36-40, 37-41, 42-46, 43-47, 44-48, 45-49, 25-50.
Special album issued
    1) Insert order form valid until 31.12.83 stapled in centre fold printed on two pages. Form printed in brown
    2) Non insert order form valid until 31.12.83 without staple marks in centre fold. Form printed in brown obtained direct from Brooke Bond.
Note: Some albums issued with an erratum insert, listing errors on cards No.3 and 15 plus two album errors. Size 127 x 88mm

The Race Into Space. Size 69 x 37mm coloured numbered series of 50. Wallchart issued.
There are two printings of this set
    A) Back printed in blue original issue issued in 1971
    B) Back printed in black reprint issue issued in 1974
Special album issued with two printings
    A) Top line of 5 in price 7mm, inside back cover printers credit "The Berkshire … England" 39mm
    B) Top line of 5 in price 8mm, inside back cover printers credit "The Berkshire … England" 45mm
        1) Insert order form stapled in fold with tag on left. Form printed in black
        2) Non insert order form without tag. Form printed in black obtained direct from Brooke Bond. Number rubber stamped on back.

The Saga of Ships. Size 69 x 37mm coloured numbered series of 50. Wallchart issued.
There are two printings of this set
    A) Back printed in blue original issue issued in 1970
    B) Back printed in black reprint issue issued in 1973
Special album issued with two printings
    A) Original – Cover printed in light blue
        1) Insert order form stapled in fold with tag on left. Form printed in blue
        2) Non insert order form without tag. Form printed in blue obtained direct from Brooke Bond. Number rubber stamped on back.
    B) Reprint – Cover printed in dark blue

The Sea - Our Other World. Size 69 x 37mm coloured numbered series of 50 issued in 1974 backs printed in black. Wallchart issued.
Special album issued with two printings
    A) Original – With printers credit "Berkshire Printing" inside back cover
        1) Insert order form stapled in centre fold printed on two pages. Form printed in black
        2) Non insert order form without staple marks in centre fold. Form printed in black obtained direct from Brooke Bond. Number rubber stamped on back.
    B) Reprint – Without printers credit "Berkshire Printing" inside back cover
Note: This series was also issued by Foster Clark in Malta

The Secret Diary of Kevin Tipps. Size 89 x 63mm coloured unnumbered series of 50 issued in 1995 backs printed in black and red.
There are two printings of card December 10
    A) Text "Samatha" without the n
    B) Text "Samantha" with the n
Special album issued
        1) Insert order form valid until 31.3.96 stapled in centre fold. Form printed in black with "Kevin says Teams Junior Club is Great" offer on left hand side.
        2) Non insert order form valid until 31.3.96 without staple marks in centre fold. Form printed in black with "Kevin says Teams Junior Club is Great" offer on left hand side obtained direct from Brooke Bond.

1) January 1
2) January 9
3) January 20
4) January 28
5) February 14
6) February 17
7) February 19
8) February 20
9) February 26
10) March 18
11) March 26
12) March 31
13) April 7
14) April 8
15) April 16
16) April 18
17) April 23
18) May 2
19) May 10
20) May 17
21) May 27
22) June 4
23) June 15
24) June 26
25) July 2
26) July 8
27) July 11
28) July 14
29) July 28
30) August 2
31) August 6
32) August 18
33) August 20
34) September 4
35) September 9
36) September 12
37) September 27
38) October 7
39) October 9
40) October 12
41) October 19
42) October 27
43) November 1
44) November 14
45) November 17
46) November 30
47) December 3
48) December 10
49) December 25
50) December 30

Small Wonders. Size 69 x 37mm coloured numbered series of 40. Wallchart issued.
There are two printings of this set
    A) Back printed in blue original issue issued in 1981
    B) Back printed in black reprint issue issued in 1988
Special album issued
        1) Insert order form valid until 30.10.82 stapled in centre fold printed on two pages. Form printed in blue
        2) Non insert order form valid until 30.10.82 without staple marks in centre fold. Form printed in blue obtained direct from Brooke Bond.

Teenage Mutant HeroTurtles - Dimension Xescapade. Coloured numbered issued in 1991 backs printed in green.
There are two printings of this set
    A) Set of 40 size 69 x 37mm one picture per card
    B) Set of 20 size 69 x 74mm two pictures per card numbered consecutively 1-2, 3-4, etc
Special album issued
    1) Insert order form valid until 31.7.91 stapled in centre fold printed in green
    2) Non insert order form valid until 31.7.91 without staple marks in centre fold. Form printed in green obtained direct from Brooke Bond.
    3) Non insert order form valid until 31.10.91 without staple marks in centre fold. Form printed in red obtained direct from Brooke Bond
    4) Non insert order form valid until 31.12.91 without staple marks in centre fold. Form printed in dark brown obtained direct from Brooke Bond

30 Years of the Chimps 1956-1986. Size 69 x 37mm coloured unnumbered series of 12 issued in 1986.
There are three printings of this set
    A) Plain back thick card with a peel off back revealing a sticky surface
    B) Plain back paper thin card with a peel off back revealing a sticky surface
    C) Back with "Taktik" randomly printed on back in blue with a peel off back revealing a sticky surface
Special album issued
    Non insert order form printed in orange valid until 31.12.86 obtained direct from Brooke Bond

1) ADA
2) AL B BLOWED
3) BROOKE BOND
4) CYRIL THE CYCLIST
5) DOLLY
6) I BODGIT
7) JEAN-PIERRE BERKE
8) MR SHIFTER
9) S BEND
10) TANIA
11) THE JUDGE
12) THE TWINS

Transport Through The Ages. Size 69 x 37mm coloured numbered series of 50. Wallchart issued.
There are two printings of this set
    A) Back printed in blue original issue issued in 1966
    B) Back printed in black reprint issue issued in 1973
Special album issued
    Original album Great Britain issue
        1) Insert order form tag on left hand side. Printed in red
        2) Insert order form tag on right hand side. Printed in red
        3) Non insert order form with no tag obtained direct from Brooke Bond. Printed in red.
Note: There was no reprint album issued.
Note: Musgrave Brooke Bond album with Musgrave on front cover. (See Issues of Musgrave-Brooke Bond Ireland)

Trees in Britain. Size 69 x 37mm coloured numbered series of 50. Wallchart issued
There are two printings of this set
- A) Back printed in blue original issue issued in 1966
- B) Back printed in black reprint issue issued in 1973

Special album issued with five printings
- A) Original – Matt cover. Text on number 15 2nd paragraph with letter T "Chestnut"
- B) Original – Matt cover. Text on number 15 2nd paragraph without letter T "Chesnut"
    1) Insert order form tag on left hand side. Printed in blue
    2) Insert order form tag on right hand side. Printed in blue
    3) Non insert order form with no tag obtained direct from Brooke Bond. Printed in blue. Number rubber stamped on back
- C) Reprint – Glossy cover with price with printers credit "Berkshire Printing" on inside back cover
- D) Reprint – Glossy cover with price without printers credit "Berkshire Printing" on inside back cover
- E) Reprint – Glossy cover without price with printers credit "Berkshire Printing" on inside back cover

Tropical Birds. Size 69 x 37mm coloured numbered series of 50.
There are two printings of this set
- A) Back printed in blue original issue issued in 1961
- B) Back printed in black reprint issue issued in 1974

Special album issued with four printings
- A) Original – Matt cover with price with printers credit "Berkshire Printing" on inside back cover
    1) Insert order form with rectangular tag on left folded downwards sloping inwards from form. Printed in red
    2) Insert order form with rectangular tag on left folded downwards sloping outwards from form. Printed in red.
    3) Insert order form with round tag on left. Printed in red.
    4) Non insert order form with no tag obtained direct from Brooke Bond. Printed in red.
- B) Reprint – Glossy cover with price with printers credit "Berkshire Printing" inside back cover
- C) Reprint – Glossy cover without price without printers credit "Berkshire Printing" inside back cover
- D) Reprint - Glossy cover without price with printers credit "Berkshire Printing" inside back cover

Note: Southern Rhodesia & East Africa album front cover without price, but red line under "C. F. Tunnicliffe, R. A.", back cover also differs from Great Britain issue with no text underneath Brooke Bond in oval.

Unexplained Mysteries of the World. Coloured numbered issued in 1987 backs printed in blue.
There are two printings of this set
- A) Set of 40 size 69 x 37mm one picture per card
- B) Set of 20 size 69 x 74mm two pictures per card numbered consecutively 1-2, 3-4, etc

Special album issued
   Insert order form loose not stapled form printed in purple valid until 31.12.87

Vanishing Wildlife. Size 69 x 37mm coloured numbered series of 40. Wallchart issued.
There are two printings of this set
    A) Back printed in brown original issue issued in 1978
    B) Back printed in black reprint issue issued in 1988
Special album issued with two printings with insert order form.
    A) Original – Matt inside cover
        1) Insert order form valid until 31.7.79 stapled in centre fold printed on two pages. Form printed in blue
        2) Non insert order form valid until 31.7.79 without staple marks in centre fold. Form printed in blue obtained direct from Brooke Bond.
        3) Non insert order form without staple marks in centre fold printed on two pages. Form printed in blue but plain back obtained direct from Brooke Bond
    B) Reprint – Glossy inside cover

Wild Birds in Britain. Size 69 x 37mm coloured numbered series of 50. Wallchart issued
There are two printings of this set
    A) Back printed in blue original issue issued in 1965
    B) Back printed in black reprint issue issued in 1973
Special album issued with three printings
    A) Original – Matt cover with price
        1) Insert order form tag on left hand side. Printed in black
        2) Insert order form tag on right hand side. Printed in black
    B) Reprint – Glossy cover with price
    C) Reprint – Glossy cover without price

Wild Flowers Series 1. Size 69 x 37mm coloured numbered series of 50 issued in 1955. Backs printed in blue.
There are two printings of this set
    A) Thick card
    B) Paper thin card
Special album issued with two printings (no insert order form).
        A) Cover with price (first printing)
        B) Cover without price (second printing)

Wild Flowers Series 2. Size 69 x 37mm coloured numbered series of 50.
There are three printings of this set
    A) Back printed in blue with "Brooke Bond Tea Ltd" original issue issued in 1959 (first printing)
    B) Back printed in blue with "Issued by Brooke Bond Tea Ltd" original issue issued in 1959 (second printing)
    C) Back printed in black reprint issue in 1973
Special album issued with three printings
    A) Original – Matt cover with price
    B) Reprint – Glossy cover with price
    C) Reprint – Glossy cover without price
Note: Album order form issued, obtained direct from Brooke Bond not published in the album. Printed in colour.

Wild Flowers Series 3. Size 69 x 37mm coloured numbered series of 50 issued in 1964 backs printed in blue. Wallchart issued.
Special album issued
        1) Insert order form tag on top with text facing left printed in red
        2) Insert order form tag on top with text facing right printed in red

Wildlife in Danger. Size 69 x 37mm coloured numbered series of 50. Wallchart issued.
There are two printings of this set
    A) Back printed in blue original issue issued in 1963
    B) Back printed in black reprint issue issued in 1973
Special album issued with three printings
    A) Original – Matt cover with price, words "British National Appeal" on page one in one line
        1) Insert order form tag on top with text facing left printed in green
        2) Insert order form tag on top with text facing right printed in green
        3) Insert order form tag on left printed in black
    B) Reprint – Glossy cover with price, words "British National Appeal" on page one in two lines
    C) Reprint – Glossy cover without price, words "British National Appeal" on page one in two lines
Note: East African album, cover with "PRICE NINEPENCE" and Southern Rhodesia album, cover with "Price 50 cents". (See Issues of Southern Rhodesia & East Africa)

The Wonderful World of Kevin Tipps. Size 89 x 63mm coloured numbered series of 30 issued in 1997 backs printed in black. Special album issued (no insert order form).
    1) Non insert order form valid until 30.4.98. Form printed in black obtained direct from Brooke Bond
    2) Non insert order form valid until 30.4.98. but with "Pyramid Power Full set of Picture Cards & Matching Album @ £1.70" marked N/A. Form printed in black obtained direct from Brooke Bond

Wonders of Wildlife. Size 69 x 37mm coloured numbered series of 50 issued in 1976 backs printed in black. Wallchart issued.
Two printings of card number 1 and 37
    No 1 A) Top to left with text upright
              B) Top to right with text upright
    No 37 A) Normal picture head at top
              B) Inverted picture head at bottom of card
Special album issued
    1) Insert order form stapled in centre fold printed on two pages. Form printed in blue
    2) Non insert order form as above but number rubber stamped on back obtained direct from Brooke Bond.
Separate 2 page insert titled "2 Ways to see the Wonders of Wildlife" issued in the album

Woodland Wildlife. Size 69 x 37mm coloured numbered series of 40. Wallchart issued.
There are two printings of this set
    A) Back printed in green original issue issued in 1980
    B) Back printed in black reprint issue issued in 1988
Special album issued.
    1) Insert order form valid until 31.8.81 stapled in centre fold printed on two pages. Form printed in grey-green
    2) Non insert order form valid until 30.9.81 without staple marks in centre fold. Form printed in grey-green obtained direct from Brooke Bond.

A SERIES OF 50   No. 42

ADVENTURERS & EXPLORERS

Written by Tim Severin
Illustrated by John Beswick

Sir Edmund Percival Hillary 1919-
Norgay Tenzing 1914-
Illustrated: Tenzing on the summit of Everest.

The first men to climb Mount Everest, Hillary, a New Zealander, and Tenzing, a Sherpa (a Tibetan hill people), were the final assault party of the 1953 British Everest expedition. Using oxygen, they reached the South summit at 11.30 am May 29. There Hillary took Tenzing's photograph, and Tenzing left a small religious offering, some sweets and a packet of biscuits. In 1957-8 Hillary led one section of the Commonwealth Trans-Antarctic Expedition, and became the first man after Scott (see card 35) to reach the South Pole overland.

Save all your cards in the full-story picture album—50 from grocers or from, Brooke Bond Oxo Ltd, Leon House, High Street, Croydon CR9 1JQ, Surrey

CARDS ISSUED WITH ALL BROOKE BOND TEA AND TEA BAGS

A SERIES OF 50.   No. 44

AFRICAN WILD LIFE

Illustrated and described by
C. F. Tunnicliffe, R.A.

ELEPHANT
(*Loxodonta africana*)

An adult male African Elephant may weigh six tons and measure eleven feet at the shoulder. In spite of its size it can move through bush and forest amazingly quietly. Elephants have acute senses of smell and hearing but their eyes are not so efficient. The trunk is a versatile fifth limb; it is a scenting organ, a hand for tearing away leaves and branches, a squirt for spraying water when bathing, and a duster for blowing sand over the body. The tusks are used as digging implements for obtaining roots in addition to being weapons of defence. Elephants are entirely vegetarian, and their tempers are unpredictable.

GET A PICTURE CARD ALBUM FROM YOUR GROCER—Price 6d

Issued in all packets of
BROOKE BOND TEA

35 Cannon Street, London, E.C.4

A SERIES OF 50.   No. 44

AFRICAN WILD LIFE

Illustrated and described by
C. F. Tunnicliffe, R.A.

ELEPHANT
(*Loxodonta africana*)

An adult male African Elephant may weigh six tons and measure eleven feet at the shoulder. In spite of its size it can move through bush and forest amazingly quietly. Elephants have acute senses of smell and hearing but their eyes are not so efficient. The trunk is a versatile fifth limb; it is a scenting organ, a hand for tearing away leaves and branches, a squirt for spraying water when bathing, and a duster for blowing sand over the body. The tusks are used as digging implements for obtaining roots in addition to being weapons of defence. Elephants are entirely vegetarian, and their tempers are unpredictable.

GET A PICTURE CARD ALBUM FROM YOUR GROCER—Price 6d

Issued in all packets of
BROOKE BOND TEA

35 Cannon Street, London, E.C.4

A SERIES OF 50.   No. 43

ASIAN WILD LIFE

Illustrated and described by
C. F. Tunnicliffe, R.A.

ASIATIC ELEPHANT
(*Elephas maximus*)

India, Ceylon, Assam, Burma, Thailand, Sumatra and Borneo are the countries of the wild Asiatic Elephant. In undulating forest country, particularly where bamboos flourish, they live in herds, keeping to the dense forest near water during the hot period of the year, but venturing into more open land in the rainy season to feed on the young grass. Elephants are entirely vegetarian in their food. They are fond of water and are excellent swimmers. At all times they are temperamental and usually shy, but old solitary bulls, and females with calves are often dangerous. An adult male will weigh between 2½ and 3 tons and average a height of 9 feet at the shoulders.

GET A PICTURE CARD ALBUM FROM YOUR GROCER—Price 6d

Issued in all packets of
BROOKE BOND TEA

35 Cannon Street, London, E.C.4

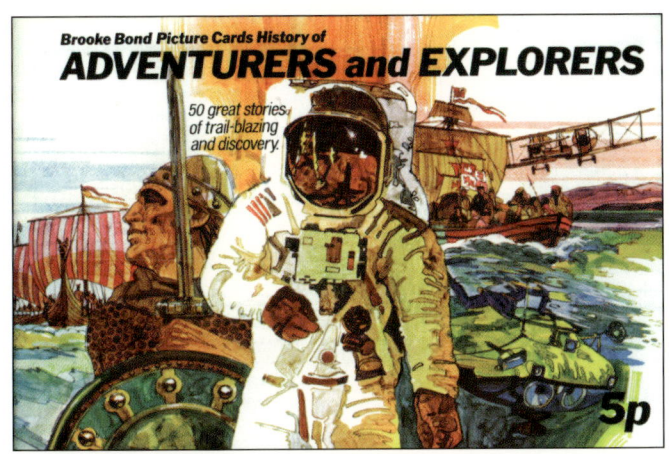

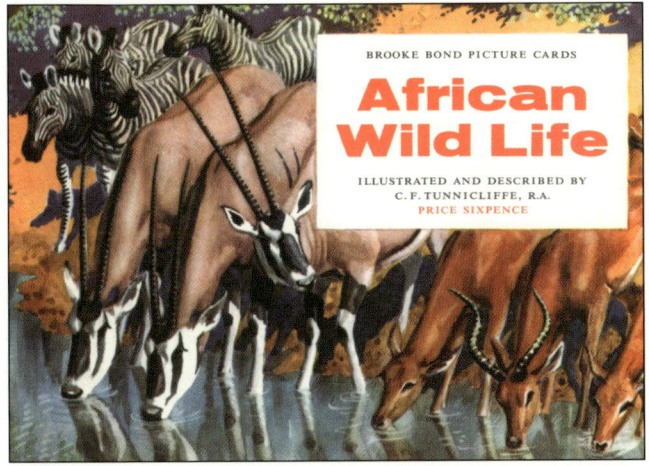

BRITISH COSTUME

Illustrated by Michael Youens
Described by Madeleine Ginsburg
of the Victoria and Albert Museum

DAY CLOTHES 1825

This illustration from a fashion plate of 1825 shows the lady's dress assuming a new outline. The waist has dropped to natural level and sleeves and skirt are wide and full. The colours are bright, trimmings elaborate and much jewellery is worn. Accessories are varied, the most noticeable is the vast hat trimmed with many ribbon bows. The man wears elegant walking dress also with a slight fullness at the shoulder and a waistcoat with lapels. He wears tight pantaloons acceptable for day wear after about 1805 and carries a higher 'top' hat.

GET A PICTURE CARD ALBUM FROM YOUR GROCER—Price 6d

Issued with **BROOKE BOND TEA** and Tea Bags

Heathrow House, Cranford, Middx.

BRITISH WILD LIFE

Described by Frances Pitt
Illustrated by C. F. Tunnicliffe, R.A.

THE YELLOW-NECKED MOUSE
(*Apodemus flavicollis wintoni*)

In many parts of the west of England, in the midland and southern counties, we meet with a large and very beautiful long-tailed or wood mouse. To country folk it is known as the greyhound mouse and to scientists as *Apodemus flavicollis wintoni*, the yellow-necked mouse of de Winton. It owes its name to a fawn band across its chest. It was first recognised as a British species in Herefordshire, our form being slightly different from the yellow-necked mouse found on the Continent.

GET A PICTURE CARD ALBUM FROM YOUR GROCER—Price 6d.

ISSUED IN PACKETS OF BROOKE BOND CHOICEST P.G. TIPS & EDGLETS TEAS

Brooke Bond & Co. Ltd.

BUTTERFLIES OF THE WORLD

Illustrated and described by Richard Ward

Delias harpalyce
PIERIDAE
(Imperial White)

The Imperial White comes from southern Australia. In New South Wales it lives in the mountains, but in Victoria is found at sea level. This butterfly earned its name from the way it soars and glides around the tops of high gum trees though it is also seen flying up and down among small streams rather in the manner of swallows. The female is greenish-white with very broad black margins. The food plant is mistletoe. Wingspan approx. 2½ inches.

GET A PICTURE CARD ALBUM FROM YOUR GROCER—Price 6d

Issued with **BROOKE BOND TEA** Crown Cup Instant Coffee

35 Cannon Street, London, E.C.4

CREATURES OF LEGEND
WITH KEVIN TIPPS
11. CYCLOPS

- In early Greek myths there were just three Cyclops, who worked in the blacksmith's forges beneath Mount Etna, an active volcano.
- They gave the weapons of thunder and lightning to the god Zeus.
- In later stories Cyclops were described as very ugly giants. Each had a single glittering eye in the middle of his forehead, beneath a bushy eyebrow.
- They were well known for their bad manners. Living on the coast of Sicily, they killed and ate any passing strangers.
- One Cyclops held the Greek traveller Odysseus prisoner. To escape, Odysseus got the Cyclops drunk and then blinded him by driving a stake into his one eye.

Never mind one eye in the forehead. Mum's got two in the back of her head!

Illustration: Mark Longworth

Special album or wallchart for 24 picture cards, just send 50p (p&p) & name and address to: Picture Card Dept. (B49), PO Box 100, Burnley, Lancs BB11 1PG. UK residents only.

THE DINOSAUR TRAIL
WITH KEVIN TIPPS
1. MASSOSPONDYLUS
'Massive Vertebra'
Lived during the Triassic age
200 -210 million years ago

Look out! This hefty monster was a real slash and grab expert! The long vicious claws on its thumb meant trouble for even the fiercest attackers. Massospondylus (mass-oh-spon-die-lus) was one of the earliest dinosaurs. It had a large, bulky body with a tiny head and grew up to 6m in length. With its small, sharp teeth, it probably had a mixed diet – mainly plants with some tasty insects for variety. The thumb claw would have also been very useful for digging and grabbing at trees so it could eat the leaves.

Illustration: John Sibbick

Special album or wallchart for your 20 Picture Cards: Just send 50p (p&p) & name and address to: Picture Card Dept. Dinosaur Trail, PO Box 100 Burnley Lancs BB1 1 1PG. UK residents only.

THE DINOSAUR TRAIL
WITH KEVIN TIPPS
1. MASSOSPONDYLUS
'Massive Vertebra'
Lived during the Triassic age
200 -210 million years ago

Look out! This hefty monster was a real slash and grab expert! The long vicious claws on its thumb meant trouble for even the fiercest attackers. Massospondylus (mass-oh-spon-die-lus) was one of the earliest dinosaurs. It had a large, bulky body with a tiny head and grew up to 6m in length. With its small, sharp teeth, it probably had a mixed diet – mainly plants with some tasty insects for variety. The thumb claw would have also been very useful for digging and grabbing at trees so it could eat the leaves.

Illustration: John Sibbick

Special album or wallchart for your 20 Picture Cards: Just send 50p (p&p) & name and address to: Picture Card Dept. Dinosaur Trail, PO Box 100 Burnley Lancs BB1 1 1PG. UK residents only.

Discovering our COAST
A SERIES OF 50

46. Blackpool (Lancashire)

Blackpool was Britain's most popular holiday resort for nearly 100 years. Donkey rides, fish and chips, 'kiss-me-quick' and the illuminations along the front are what Blackpool still means to most. Generations of North-country comics have kept this powerful image going, and even the changing holiday scene cannot erase the picture. While more people now take holidays abroad, Blackpool has become a major conference centre, with the famous Blackpool Tower now symbolising the annual Party Conferences. Built in 1894, the 158-metre Tower was for years the highest building in Britain. Housing a circus, ballroom and aquarium, bars and restaurants and an Educational Heritage Exhibition, this famous landmark can be seen from as far as the Lake District to the north and Snowdonia in the south-west.

Photograph: Spectrum

Special Album or Wallchart for your 50 Picture Cards: just send 2 × 20p coins (p&p) plus your name, address and choice of item to: Brooke Bond Oxo Ltd., Picture Card Dept. DC, PO Box 216, Croydon CR9 5TL.

Discovering our COAST
A SERIES OF 50

46. Blackpool (Lancashire)

Blackpool was Britain's most popular holiday resort for nearly 100 years. Donkey rides, fish and chips, 'kiss-me-quick' and the illuminations along the front are what Blackpool still means to most. Generations of North-country comics have kept this powerful image going, and even the changing holiday scene cannot erase the picture. While more people now take holidays abroad, Blackpool has become a major conference centre, with the famous Blackpool Tower now symbolising the annual Party Conferences. Built in 1894, the 158-metre Tower was for years the highest building in Britain. Housing a circus, ballroom and aquarium, bars and restaurants and an Educational Heritage Exhibition, this famous landmark can be seen from as far as the Lake District to the north and Snowdonia in the south-west.

Photograph: Spectrum

Special Album or Wallchart for your 50 Picture Cards: just send 2 × 20p coins (p&p) plus your name, address and choice of item to: Brooke Bond Oxo Ltd., Picture Card Dept. DC, PO Box 216, Croydon CR9 5TL.

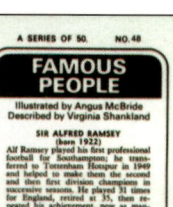

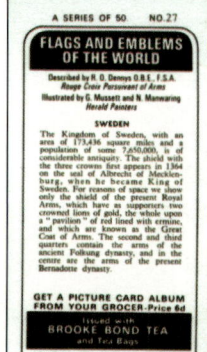

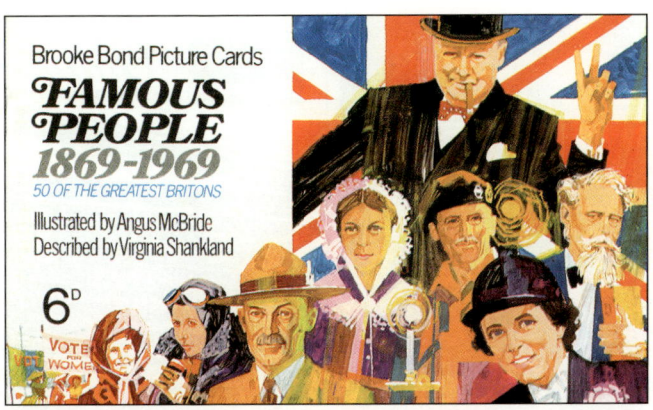

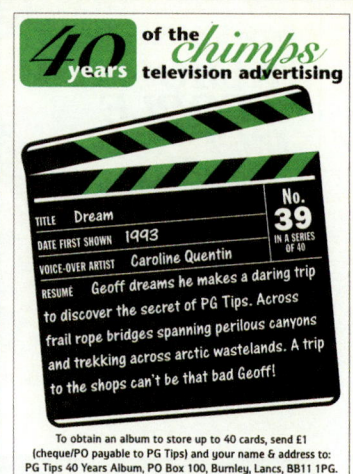

INCREDIBLE CREATURES

IN THE SEA
A Series of 40 Cards

12. Deep-Sea Jellyfish

Deep-sea jellyfish are tiny, beautiful creatures that look like miniature space-ships. As their name suggests, they live at considerable depths under the sea, 10 kilometres or more below the surface, where it is completely dark and very cold. The deeper they live, the more brightly-coloured they are. Their 'umbrellas', which are about 5 centimetres across, can be bright blue, red, pink or any other colour. Very few people have been fortunate enough to see deep-sea jellyfish because they very rarely come near the surface.

Save your 40 picture cards together in a set of 4 wall charts.
Just send 2 x 20p coins, plus your name and address to: Brooke Bond Oxo Ltd., Dept. 1C, Parkway House, Sheen Lane, London SW14 8LU.

1 INTERNATIONAL SOCCER STARS

Name: Teddy Sheringham
Country: England
D.O.B.: 02/04/66
Height: 6'0"
Club: Manchester United, England

An inspired signing by Alex Ferguson to replace Eric Cantona, Teddy Sheringham was an instant success for Manchester United both scoring and creating goals for others.

Brooke Bond
PG Tips

To obtain a great album (to store up to 20 cards) with a wallchart, simply send just £2 (cheque/Postal Order made payable to PG Tips) with your name and address to: PG Tips Soccer Stars Album and Wallchart Offer, PO Box 100, Burnley, Lancs. BB11 1PG. UK only. Allow 28 days for delivery.

A SERIES OF 50   No. 20

Inventors & Inventions

Written by Ken Roscoe
Illustrated by Barry Rowe

George Stephenson's 'Rocket', 1829
The Stephensons—George, and Robert his son—were undoubtedly the fathers of the modern efficient steam train, although engineers such as Trevithick had had some success earlier. George Stephenson's first locomotive, in 1814, pulled several trucks at four mph. His second engine marked a milestone—it forced the exhaust steam up the chimney and so greatly increased the draught for the fire. His engine 'Locomotion No. 1' opened the world's first fare-paying railway for freight and passengers, between Stockton and Darlington. His 'Rocket', four years later, easily won the important Rainhill Trials. One of the 'Rocket's' competitors was disqualified, as its 'engine' was a horse on a treadmill.

Save all your cards in the full-story picture album—free grocers or from: Brooke Bond Oxo Ltd, Leon House, High Street, Croydon CR9 1JQ, Surrey

CARDS ISSUED WITH ALL BROOKE BOND TEA AND TEA BAGS

· A JOURNEY · DOWNSTREAM
A SERIES OF 25

6. THE OTTER
Otters have streamlined, fur covered bodies about 1m long with short legs, a thick tail and small ears. They are largely nocturnal and live near undisturbed rivers, streams, lakes and coasts. They use up to 40km of riverbank as a home range, and depend on clean water, bankside cover and a plentiful supply of fish, especially eels. Their prey is caught during short dives.
Breeding may occur at any time during the year. Between 1 and 4 cubs are born in a holt (den) and stay with the mother for about a year.
The otter population has declined over the last 30 years. They are now rare or absent in much of Britain and are protected by law. Likely causes of the decline are pesticides and habitat loss. The RSNC's Otters and Rivers Project is working hard to protect otters and their habitat in England and Wales. This picture card series is dedicated to supporting the project.

Special Album for your 25 Picture Cards: Just send cheque/PO for 70p made payable to Brooke Bond Foods Ltd (which includes 20p donation to RSNC Otters & Rivers Project) plus name and address to: Picture Card Dept. JD, PO Box 216, Croydon CR9 3TL. UK residents only.

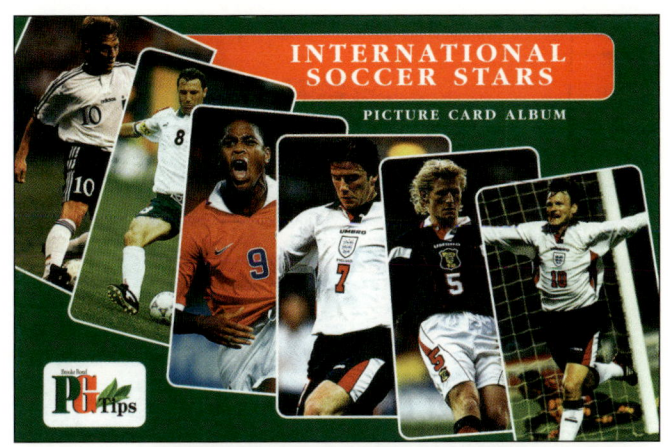

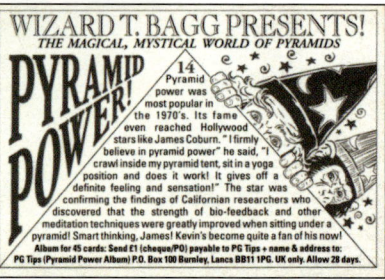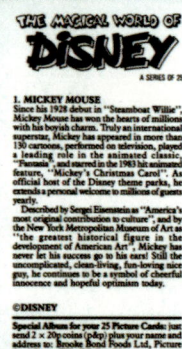

No Album issued for The Language Tea

NATURAL NEIGHBOURS
Wildlife in tea-growing lands
A SERIES OF 40

18. GIRAFFE
The giraffe, with its distinctive long neck, tall legs and blotched coat is the world's tallest animal. A mature bull may be 5.4m tall. Males live apart from females who graze with their young, and are visited by males at mating times. They browse on trees and bushes (acacia is a favourite), and can go without water for long intervals. Calves can be born at any time of year, and can walk within an hour of birth.
Photograph: Bruce Coleman Limited

Special album or wallchart for your 40 Picture Cards: just send £1 (p&p) to Brooke Bond Foods Ltd (40p of which is helping to raise funds for World Wide Fund for Nature) plus name and address to: Picture Card Dept. WWF, P.O. Box 100, Burnley, Lancs. BB11 1PG
UK residents only.

OLYMPIC
challenge 1992
A Series of 40 Cards

18. DALEY THOMPSON (GB)
Flamboyant personality who equalled Bob Mathias' record of winning two decathlon Golds. In Moscow, 1980, he was at the height of his powers and was not seriously threatened, receiving a standing ovation as he finished the final event, the 1,500 metres. In Los Angeles, 1984, he did battle with world record holder Jurgen Hingsen, the cut-and-thrust of their duel proving to be an absorbing battle of speed and strength. For Seoul, 1988, he was returning from injury and was not at his best, but still finished fourth.
Photograph: Allsport/Steve Powell

Special Album or Wallchart for your 40 Picture Cards: just send £1 (p&p) to Brooke Bond Foods Ltd (40p of which is helping to raise funds for the British Olympic Team) plus your name and address to: Picture Card Dept. OC, P.O. Box 100, Burnley, Lancs. BB11 1PG.
UK residents only.

No.35
RODNEY PATTISSON
5.8.1943 —
GT. BRITAIN & NI
YACHTING
2 GOLD; 1 SILVER
Scottish-born Rodney Pattisson triumphed in the 1968 Olympic 'Flying Dutchman' class in 'Super...docious'. Winning five races out of the six to count and finishing second in the other, he incurred the lowest number of penalty points in the annals of Olympic yachting. Four years later Pattisson retained the title with 'Superdoso', in 1976 he struck silver, and in 1980 he will try for a third gold.

 Save all 40 cards in this series on a wallchart or in an album. You can obtain either by sending a 10p coin to: Brooke Bond Oxo Ltd., Dept. OG, Parkway House, Sheen Lane, London SW14 8LU.

No.35
RODNEY PATTISSON
5.8.1943 —
GT. BRITAIN & NI
YACHTING
2 GOLD; 1 SILVER
Scottish-born Rodney Pattisson triumphed in the 1968 Olympic 'Flying Dutchman' class in 'Super...docious'. Winning five races out of the six to count and finishing second in the other, he incurred the lowest number of penalty points in the annals of Olympic yachting. Four years later Pattisson retained the title with 'Superdoso', in 1976 he struck silver, and in 1980 he will try for a third gold.

 Save all 40 cards in this series on a wallchart or in an album. You can obtain either by sending a 10p coin to: Brooke Bond Oxo Ltd., Dept. OG, Parkway House, Sheen Lane, London SW14 8LU.

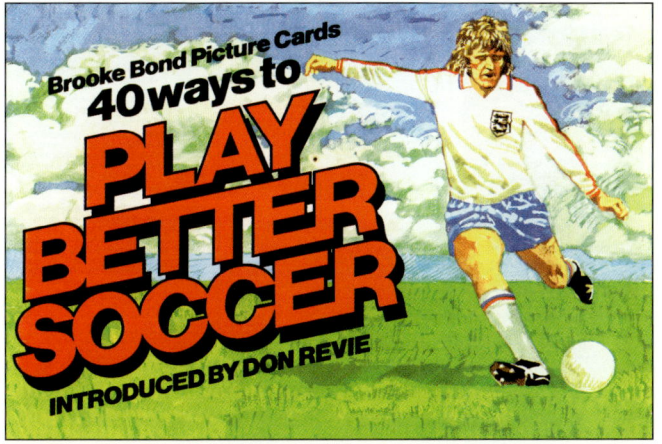

No. 37
SNOW FLAKE
Crystal formation

The snow flakes we see falling to the ground are made of many microscopic snow crystals. These crystals form in snow clouds when there is no wind and the temperature is near freezing. The breathtaking beauty of the symmetrical hexagonal (six-sided) crystals can be seen only by looking down a microscope. Since no two crystals are identical, the shape of each one can tell scientists about the air currents and temperatures which it passed through on its journey to the ground.

FREE album or poster, just send 15p (10p and 5p coins only) for postage with your name and address to:- Brooke Bond Oxo Limited, Picture Card Department SW, Parkway House, Sheen Lane, London SW14 8LU.

No. 37
SNOW FLAKE
Crystal formation

The snow flakes we see falling to the ground are made of many microscopic snow crystals. These crystals form in snow clouds when there is no wind and the temperature is near freezing. The breathtaking beauty of the symmetrical hexagonal (six-sided) crystals can be seen only by looking down a microscope. Since no two crystals are identical, the shape of each one can tell scientists about the air currents and temperatures which it passed through on its journey to the ground.

FREE album or poster, just send 15p (10p and 5p coins only) for postage with your name and address to:- Brooke Bond Oxo Limited, Picture Card Department SW, Parkway House, Sheen Lane, London SW14 8LU.

DIMENSION X ESCAPADE
A SERIES OF 12

12. MICHAELANGELO

This Hero Turtle wears orange and is a wild prankster. A mean fighter with a big smile, he chases parties and pizzas with real determination.

Michaelangelo tries to mix fighting with fun and usually ends up in a radical mess!
FACTFILE. Before helping to create The Teenage Mutant Hero Turtles, Peter Laird was a freelance artist. At the time of his success, he was drawing flowers for the gardening page of a newspaper.

© 1990 Mirage Studios. Licensed by Copyright Promotions Ltd

Special Album for your 12 Picture Cards: just send 3 x 20p coins (p&p) plus your name and address to: Brooke Bond Picture Card Dept: DE, PO Box 64, Maidenhead SL6 1HS.

BROOKE BOND

Nostradamus

Michel de Nostredame (1503-1566) was a physician, counsellor and astrologer to two French kings. He is better known as Nostradamus, whose prophesies have tantalised every generation since 1555.

His complex four-line verses, filled with vague allusions and plays on words, are drawn from at least seven languages. They are said to foretell momentous events like the Great Fire of London, the rise of the French Republic, World War I, the rise of Hitler and Mussolini, and the end of the world in 2000 AD.

One prophecy was very specific. Nostradamus gave the exact circumstances of his death, including who would find him and where. It came true.

Illustration: Edimedia

Save your 40 picture cards in a special album. Just send 2 × 20p coins plus your name and address to:
Brooke Bond Picture Card Dept.,
PO Box 216, Croydon CR9 5TA

Vanishing Wildlife

No. 15
Malayan Tapir
Area: Thailand to Sumatra
Status: Endangered

The Malayan tapir depends for its survival on swampy low-lying forest with open banks on the edge of streams. This habitat is fast being destroyed in Asia. The tapir is rather solitary and unsociable, and cannot tolerate disturbance by man; as a result, its numbers are declining everywhere. This tapir is an excellent swimmer and is said to be able to walk along the bottom of a stream like a hippopotamus.

Save all 40 cards in this series on a wallchart or in an album. You can obtain either by sending in a second class postage stamp to:
Brooke Bond Oxo Ltd,
Dept. VW, Parkway House, Sheen Lane,
London SW14 8LU.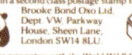

Compiled in association with the World Wildlife Fund

Vanishing Wildlife

No. 15
Malayan Tapir
Area: Thailand to Sumatra
Status: Endangered

The Malayan tapir depends for its survival on swampy low-lying forest with open banks on the edge of streams. This habitat is fast being destroyed in Asia. The tapir is rather solitary and unsociable, and cannot tolerate disturbance by man; as a result, its numbers are declining everywhere. This tapir is an excellent swimmer and is said to be able to walk along the bottom of a stream like a hippopotamus.

Save all 40 cards in this series on a wallchart or in an album. You can obtain either by sending in a second class postage stamp to:
Brooke Bond Oxo Ltd,
Dept. VW, Parkway House, Sheen Lane,
London SW14 8LU.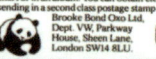

Compiled in association with the World Wildlife Fund

A SERIES OF 50. No. 11

WILD BIRDS IN BRITAIN

Illustrated and described by C.F. Tunnicliffe R.A.

WHINCHAT
(*Saxicola rubetra*)

The sprightly Whinchat is a summer visitor to Britain, appearing about mid-April and leaving us again in September or early October to winter in tropical Africa. It is a haunter of heaths and rough lands, and is often seen on pastures and in railway cuttings as it hunts for beetles, wireworms, flies and other insects. The nest is placed close to the ground, in low herbage or low shrubs. It is loosely constructed of dry grass and moss and is lined with hair and fine fibres. Only the hen builds the nest while the male accompanies her. The male is depicted. Length 5 ins.

GET A PICTURE CARD ALBUM FROM YOUR GROCER—Price 6d

Issued with
BROOKE BOND TEA
Crown Cup Instant Coffee

35 Cannon Street, London, E.C.4

A SERIES OF 50. No. 11

WILD BIRDS IN BRITAIN

Illustrated and described by C.F. Tunnicliffe R.A.

WHINCHAT
(*Saxicola rubetra*)

The sprightly Whinchat is a summer visitor to Britain, appearing about mid-April and leaving us again in September or early October to winter in tropical Africa. It is a haunter of heaths and rough lands, and is often seen on pastures and in railway cuttings as it hunts for beetles, wireworms, flies and other insects. The nest is placed close to the ground, in low herbage or low shrubs. It is loosely constructed of dry grass and moss and is lined with hair and fine fibres. Only the hen builds the nest while the male accompanies her. The male is depicted. Length 5 ins.

GET A PICTURE CARD ALBUM FROM YOUR GROCER—Price 6d

Issued with
BROOKE BOND TEA
Crown Cup Instant Coffee

35 Cannon Street, London, E.C.4

60

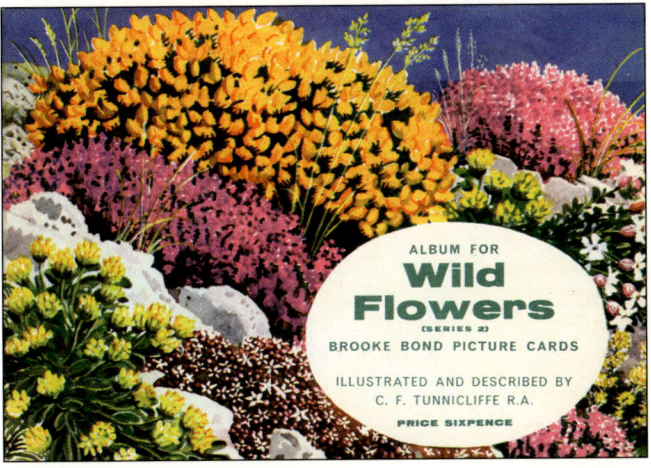

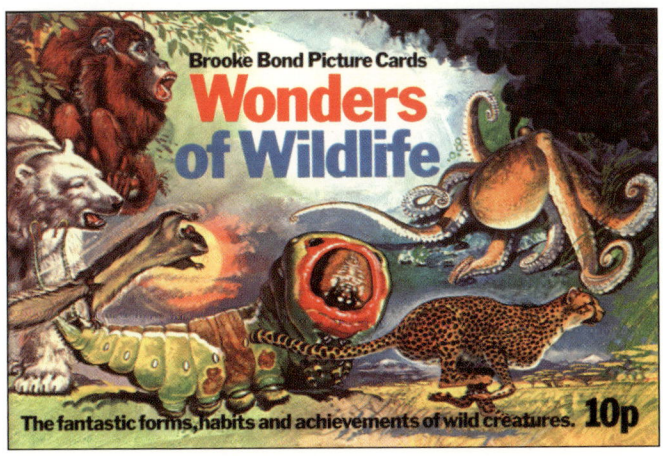

Woodland Wildlife

No. 22
FOX

Common habitat:
Woodlands, rocky outcrops, sea cliffs.
Clever ways have enabled foxes to survive since prehistoric times. They need their skills to avoid the Hunt and will even climb trees to escape. Foxes adapt readily and are now quite common scavengers in urban areas. Their diet has changed since the disease Myxomatosis virtually eliminated rabbits. However, their food varies from insects to game and farmyard chickens, one reason for their persecution.

Observation hint:
Red coat, bushy tail, distinctive musty smell.

Free Album or Wallchart
Save all 40 cards in this series in a super Album or Wallchart. Just send a 10p coin (for postage) with your name and address to:
Brooke Bond Oxo Ltd.,
Picture Card Dept. WW,
Parkway House,
Sheen Lane, London.
SW14 8LU.

Compiled in association with The Woodland Trust.

Miscellaneous Issues

40 Years of Cards (1954 – 1994). Size 68 x 37mm coloured numbered series of 48 issued in 1994 with special presentation box, no special album issued.
There are three printings of this set
  A) Back printed in dark blue
  B) Back printed in light blue
  C) Back printed in black
Promotional card issued. Butterflies of the World front with Sample across top right hand corner size 68 x 37mm
There are two printings of this card
  A) Back printed in light blue
  B) Back printed in black
Note: This set was issued by Teams Ltd in association with Brooke Bond

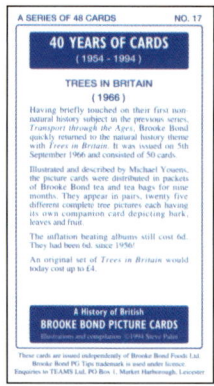 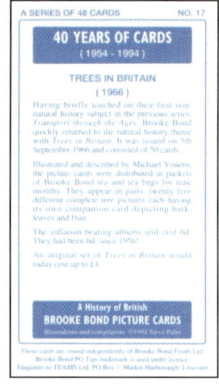 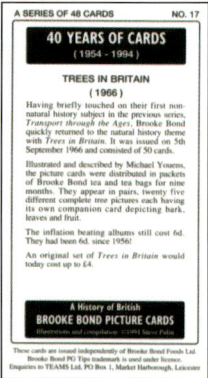

P G Tips Phonecards

Size 89 x 64mm coloured unnumbered series of 11 issued in 1998. Every card has an individual pin number and therefore no two cards are alike. The last three cards could only be obtained direct from Brooke Bond eg 21 minutes cost £2, 42 minutes cost £4 and 84 minutes cost £8

1. 3 minutes   Brrr… Brrr… Brrr
2. 3 minutes   Call me Kevin!
3. 3 minutes   I'm on my pager
4. 3 minutes   It's Nelly on a trunk call
5. 3 minutes   Just tap in your number
6. 3 minutes   Painting by numbers
7. 3 minutes   Shirley's otherwise engaged
8. 3 minutes   You answer it… no you answer it
9. 21 minutes 1,2, free minutes
10. 42 minutes Nice little number
11. 84 minutes Tell them I'm not in

Place the Face Bingo Cards.
Black and white. Unnumbered series of 15. Plain back. Issued in 1972
Four printings of this set as follows
    A) Size 68 x 37mm Single face on left:
        1) Inscribed "There are three faces in PG Tips 72 size Teabags" with Bingo logo underneath on right of card.
        2) No text. Bingo logo only on right of card
    B) Size 68 x 37mm Three faces, Bingo logo below
    C) Size 42 x 30 to 38mm irregular shape, Single face printed on flap of tea packet.

Single Face Series
1. Anthony Barber
2. Tony Blackburn
3. Richard Burton
4. Jack Charlton
5. Agatha Christie
6. Evonne Goolagong
7. Edward Heath
8. Dustin Hoffman
9. Steve McQueen
10. Paul Newman
11. Richard Nixon
12. Elvis Presley
13. Dr Spock
14. Ringo Starr
15. Elizabeth Taylor

Three Face Series

1.	Anthony Barber	Tony Blackburn	Richard Burton
2.	Anthony Barber	Jack Charlton	Edward Heath
3.	Tony Blackburn	Agatha Christie	Dustin Hoffman
4.	Tony Blackburn	Richard Nixon	Steve McQueen
5.	Richard Burton	Edward Heath	Steve McQueen
6.	Jack Charlton	Agatha Christie	Evonne Goolagong
7.	Edward Heath	Agatha Christie	Ringo Starr
8.	Edward Heath	Dustin Hoffman	Steve McQueen
9.	Dustin Hoffman	Evonne Goolagong	Elizabeth Taylor
10.	Dustin Hoffman	Richard Nixon	Ringo Starr
11.	Steve McQueen	Elvis Presley	Elizabeth Taylor
12.	Paul Newman	Evonne Goolagong	Dr Spock
13.	Paul Newman	Richard Nixon	Elvis Presley
14.	Richard Nixon	Paul Newman	Dustin Hoffman
15.	Dr Spock	Ringo Starr	Elizabeth Taylor

Note: A Place the Face Bingo leaflet was published with instructions on how to play which contained a cut out portion to stick the 15 faces.

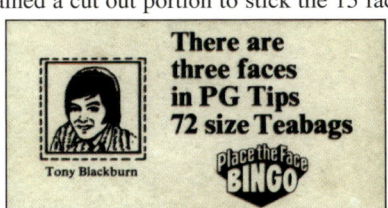

Polyfilla Modelling Cards. Size 132 x 92mm coloured numbered series of 10 issued in 1974 backs printed in black no special album issued

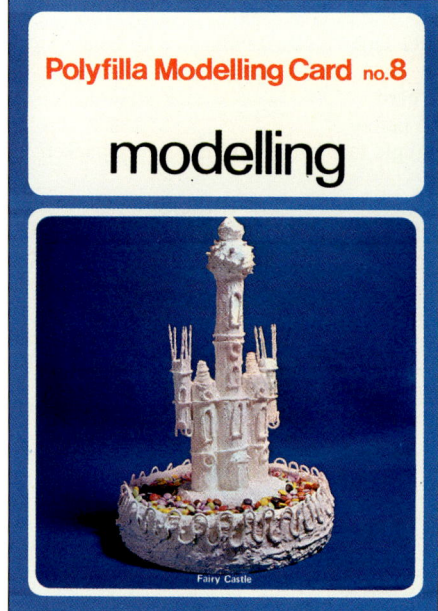
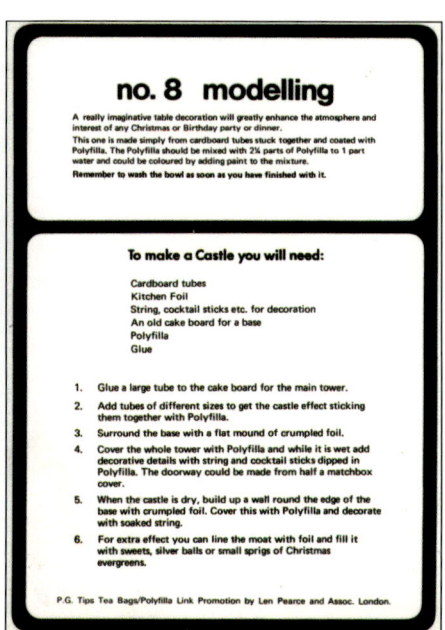

Tea Leaf Oracle.
Size 89 x 63mm. Coloured unnumbered series of 19. Issued in 1999. Cards have similar fronts with a dark brown circle in the middle of a tea cup, when heated it reveals three symbols. Cards listed by symbols as they appear reading from top to bottom

1.	Ant	Ear	Fish
2.	Ant	Telephone	Fir Tree
3.	Book	Question	Chair
4.	Bucket	Ivy	Book
5.	Dog	Ear	Robin
6	Fish	Fork	Geese
7.	Fish	Fork	Telephone
8.	Fork	Key	Chair
9.	Geese	Bucket	Ivy
10.	Jug	Dog	Ladybird
11.	Key	Bucket	Ivy
12.	Key	Question	Yew
13.	Ladybird	Jug	Fish
14.	Mouse	Question	Book
15.	Nettle	Mouse	Robin

16.	Volcano	Book	Geese
17.	Volcano	Fork	Telephone
18.	Volcano	Heart	Nettle
19.	Yew	Heart	Key

Tea Quiz Competition. Size 115 x 80mm. Coloured series of 29? Issued in 1986.
Fronts have an African Elephant on the left and details of the competition on the right. Backs with text of How to enter etc plus a box containing a question. Each card is identical except for the question box which also contains the card number.
Cards numbers known
- 15) How long does a tea bush last?
- 16) What is the source of the perfume used in Earl Grey tea?
- 17) How long must a tea bush grow before the leaves can be picked?
- 18) The Capital of Kenya is ?
- 29) Who were the first people to add milk to their tea?

Zena Skinner International Cookery. Size 102 x 63mm coloured unnumbered series of 50 issued in 1974 backs printed in black. No special album issued. These cards do not have Brooke Bond name on them but are inscribed "Recommended by Woman's Realm".

1) AUSTRIA – Wiener Schnitzel
2) BELGIUM – Flemish Beef Stew
3) CANADA – Glazed Gammon
4) DENMARK – Danish Rollmop
5) ENGLAND – Apricot Fool
6) ENGLAND – Fisherman's Pie
7) ENGLAND – Kedgeree
8) ENGLAND – Steak, Kidney & Mushroom Pie
9) ENGLAND – Welsh Rarebit
10) FRANCE – Boeuf a la Mode
11) FRANCE – Boeuf Bourguignonne
12) FRANCE – Chicken Vol au Vent
13) FRANCE – French Onion Soup
14) FRANCE – Halibut a l'Orange
15) FRANCE – Quiche Lorraine
16) FRANCE – Souffle Omelette
17) FRANCE – Stuffed Eggs
18) FRANCE – Whiting Meuniere
19) GERMANY – Black Cherry Flan
20) GERMANY – Frankfurters with Sauerkraut
21) GERMANY – Gebratener Truthahn
22) GERMANY – Salami Salad
23) GREECE – Moussaka
24) GREECE – Stuffed Cabbage Leaves
25) GREECE – Stuffed Tomatoes
26) HUNGARY – Hungarian Goulash Nests
27) HUNGARY – Veal Paprika
28) INDIA – Chicken Curry
29) INDIA – Lamb Curry
30) ITALY – Antipasto
31) ITALY – Meatballs with Tagliatelle
32) ITALY – Orange Sorbet
33) ITALY – Spaghetti con Funghi
34) ITALY – Spaghetti Milanese
35) MEDITERRANEAN – Salad Nicoise
36) POLAND – Apple Fritters
37) POLAND – Polish Lattice Flan
38) RUSSIA – Beef Stroganoff
39) RUSSIA – Stuffed Chicken Legs
40) SCOTLAND – Finnan Fish Cakes
41) SPAIN – Spanish Chicken
42) SWEDEN – Swedish Haddock Salad
43) SWITZERLAND – Muesli
44) TURKEY – Kebabs
45) U.S.A. – Chicken Maryland
46) U.S.A. – Baked Alaska
47) U.S.A. – Creole Omelette

48) U.S.A – Peach Shortcake
49) U.S.A. – Southern Lamb Chops
50) U.S.A. – Strawberry Shortcake

1966 World Cup Souvenir Booklet. 8 pages size 202 x 117mm. Coloured. Issued in 1966.

Playing Cards

British Costume – Family Card Game. Size 88 x 57mm with square corners. Coloured series of 36. Issued in 1975. Backs printed with orange background and picture of man's head with hat and ruff around his neck. The cards are anonymous but were issued in a presentation box inscribed "Happy House". The set contains 9 different pictures with 4 of each making 36.

1. 1050 Day Clothes
2. 1150 Day and Travelling Clothes
3. 1350 Day Clothes
4. 1545 Lady's Formal Dress
5. 1610 Lady's Formal Dress
6. 1780 Country Clothes
7. 1872 Day Clothes
8. 1916 Day Clothes
9. 1967 Day Clothes

Flags and Emblems – Snap. Size 88 x 57mm with square corners. Coloured series of 36. Issued in 1975. Backs printed with purple background and picture of coat of arms. The cards are anonymous but were issued in a presentation box inscribed "Happy House". The set contains 9 different pictures with 4 of each making 36.

1. Canada
2. Denmark
3. Ireland
4. Israel
5. Italy
6. Jamaica
7. Japan
8. New Zealand
9. United Kingdom

Motor History – Snap. Size 88 x 57mm with square corners. Coloured series of 36. Issued in 1975. Backs printed with blue background and picture of a car. The cards are anonymous but were issued in a presentation box inscribed "Happy House". The set contains 9 different pictures with 4 of each making 36.

1. 1903. Oldsmobile 5 H.P. Curved Dash 1.5 litres. (U.S.A.)
2. 1907. Rolls-Royce 40/50 H.P. Silver Ghost 7/7.4 litres. (G.B.)
3. 1908. Ford Model T 2.9 litres. (U.S.A.)
4. 1933. Napier-Railton Track Car 24 litres. (G.B.)
5. 1935. Volkswagen V3 Prototype 996 c.c. (Germany)
6. 1948. Jaguar XK120 3.4 litres (G.B.)
7. 1958. Vanwall Grand Prix 2.5 litres. (G.B.)
8. 1959. Morris Mini Minor Front-Wheel-Drive 848 c.c. (G.B.)
9. 1968. Jensen FF Four-Wheel-Drive 6.3 litres. (G.B.)

P G Tips Get Out! Size 87 x 57mm with rounded corners. Coloured series of 55. Backs printed with yellow background titled Get Out! except for the 3 instruction cards which have white backgrounds. Issued in presentation box in 1995.
Cards numbered as follows

GEOFF	1, 2, 3, 4, 5, 7, 8, 10, 11, 12, 13, 14
KEVIN	1, 2, 3, 5, 7, 10, 11, 13, 14
SAMANTHA	1, 2, 3, 4, 5, 7, 8, 10, 11, 12, 13, 14
SHIRLEY	1, 2, 3, 5, 7, 10, 11, 13, 14
THE TEA PICKER	1, 2, 3, 4, 5, 7, 8
GET OUT!	20, (3 cards exactly the same)

Instruction cards numbered 1/2, 3/4, 5

P G Tips Playing Cards. Size 87 x 57mm with rounded corners. Coloured series of 54 pack of 52 playing cards plus 2 jokers one in black one in red (picture of Kevin Tipps). Backs printed with green background and border with white band across centre inscribed "It's the P G Tips taste". Issued in presentation box in 1995

P G Tips Snap! Size 88 x 57mm with rounded corners. Coloured series of 36. Backs printed with green background and cream border with white band across centre inscribed "P G Tips Snap!" Issued in presentation box in 1995.
Two identical cards of each

Geoff Tipps	1)	Red jumper holding cup and saucer
	2)	Red jumper leaning on book
	3)	Blue shirt holding camera
	4)	Blue shirt head without camera
	5)	Wearing pyjamas and dressing gown
Kevin Tipps	1)	With tea cup
	2)	Holding tooth brush
	3)	Holding spoon
	4)	On skateboard
	5)	Books in foreground
Samantha Tipps	1)	With egg and spoon
	2)	Holding cup and saucer
	3)	Wearing green garment with white spots
	4)	Wearing gold top and green skirt
Shirley Tipps	1)	With P G Tips tea packet
	2)	Hand on head
	3)	Half length hand at bottom of picture
	4)	Head and shoulders leaning on wrist

P G Tips Trick Cards. Size 88 x 57mm with rounded corners. Coloured series of 55 pack of 52 playing cards plus instruction card titled Feel the Pulse/Colour by Numbers (black text only) and an extra red ace with diamonds on left and hearts on right and extra black ace with spades on left and clubs on right. Backs printed with green background and cream border with white band across centre inscribed "It's the P G Tips taste". Issued in presentation box in 1995.

Snip Snap – The Decimal Currency Game. Size 85 x 56mm. with rounded corners. Coloured. Series of 48. Issued in 1970. Backs printed in green and brown with 3 green and 3 brown circles on 3 brown and 3 green squares. The cards are anonymous but were issued in a presentation box inscribed "With the compliments of Brooke Bond Oxo Ltd." Printed with orange background. There are 22 coin cards two of each plus 4 identical rule/list cards plus a thin information sheet.

Old Pence		New Pence	
1)	1.2d	12)	½ p
2)	2.4d	13)	1p
3)	4.8d	14)	2p
4)	1/-	15)	5p
5)	2/-	16)	10p
6)	3/-	17)	15p
7)	4/-	18)	20p
8)	5/-	19)	25p
9)	10/-	20)	50p
10)	15/-	21)	75p
11)	£1	22)	£1

Note: This set was also issued without Brooke Bond name on the presentation box (Sold in shops as a general card game). The box is inscribed " Decimal Snap created by Eric Wagstaff. Made in Great Britain. Patent applied for © Michael Stanfield Holdings, London 1968 21 Jockey Fields, London WC1"

Advertisement Cards and Inserts

1960? Paper thin card with 4 orange savings stamps on top underneath "Save these stamps for gifts or cash with Brooke Bond Dividend. Pennies save you pounds." Printed in orange

1963 Why is Crown Cup "Medium Roasted"? Single card issue printed in brown size 69 x 37mm.

1963 3 Crown Cups and Saucers. Single card issue printed in red size 69 x 37mm

1964 Danish designed Tableware Set of 2 printed in black size 69 x 37mm
1) Text only headed "Special Offer!"
2) Picture of 4 pieces of cutlery with two varieties
   A) Special Offer! Selection of four beautifully….
   B) Special Offer! This lovely spoon is free.

1965 Radio London Set of 2 printed in black size 69 x 37mm
1) Are You in Range of Radio London?
2) Who am I? Competition Entry Form

1966 6-Piece Cutlery Set of 2 printed in black size 69 x 37mm
1) Picture of 6 pieces of cutlery
2) To Get Your Beautiful 6-Piece Cutlery set order form on back

1967 Free Opal Glass Jar. Single card issue printed in blue size 69 x 37mm. Text "Brooke Bond the makers of Crown Cup trust that you have enjoyed the rich flavour of our Crown Cup Instant Coffee" Text in semi oval border with ornate design on each corner. Plain back. No mention of Opal Glass Jar on card.
Note: A reprint of this card was issued in 2004 by Alan Wrathall with permission from Brooke Bond and has a text back.

1976 Play Better Soccer set and album offer. Single card issue printed in black plain back size 69 x 37mm

1976 Play Better Soccer Great New Series! Single card issue printed in red plain back size 69 x 37mm

1977 Police File New Picture Card Series. Single card issue printed in blue plain back size 69 x 37mm

1994 Token – Keep This Token Brooke Bond D. Single card issue printed in yellow and red on green background. Plain back.
There were two sizes
1) size 69 x 36mm. Single card
2) size 69 x 72mm. Double card

1994 Token Brooke Bond D 1 Token. Single card issue printed in yellow, red and green with white background. Yellow border and red frameline. Picture of stamp token on left and text on right. Plain back.

1994 The Tipps Family Transfer Kit. Single card with 10 transfers (coloured) plus a card with instructions printed in black plain back size 113 x 80mm. This was part of a PG Tips Activity Book titled Meet the Tipps family

1994 Carefully Decaffeinated. Single card issue size 78 x 47mm. Front picture of waterfall in colour, back leaf at top right, bottom PG Tips Low caffeine

1994 Brooke Bond Orange Label. Single card issue size 78 x 47mm. Front in orange back with black text

1994 Brooke Bond D Refreshing tea. Single card issue size 78 x 94mm. Front printed in green and yellow. Back with line drawing of two children sitting on mother's back.

1996 PG Tips Tipps Family 1997 Calendar. Single card issue size 89 x 63mm. Front printed in colour. Back with application form printed in black.

1999 PG Tips Need Your Help! Single card issue coloured backs printed in green and black size 89 x 63mm

1999 Thank You! Single card issue coloured size 89 x 63mm
1999 Farewell to Picture Cards. Set of 3 coloured backs printed in green and red size 89 x 63mm
  1) Plain white background with picture Kevin
  2) Coloured background with cactus and Kevin
  3) Coloured background with tree and Kevin
2001 PG Tips Bean Chimp Offer. Single card issue coloured size 89 x 68mm
  1) With multicoloured circle on right side. Back with order form
  2) With dark brown circle on right side. Back with order form
2005 Scratch Card. Are you a PG Tips 2 Go Winner? Single card issue coloured backs Send your winning scratch card …… to: Tea in Tesco iPod shuffle offer Promotion 1st Nov 2005 – 18th Dec 2005 Size 100mm x 65mm
2007 Scratch Card. Single card issue. "Why don't you scratch and see if you're a winner while I have a refreshing cup of PG Tips tea" Front coloured with picture of a knitted monkey. Back with Terms and Conditions offer of a knitted monkey promotion 5th February to 28th October 2007 Size 60mm x 40mm.

Official Reference Books

1st Edition 1954 – 1966 (40 pages)
  1967 Addendum 11 pages with Trees in Britain, Flags and Emblems of the World plus details of Canada & USA, South Africa, Musgrave Brooke Bond issues
2nd Edition 1954 – 1967 (48 pages)
3rd Edition 1954 – 1968 (52 pages)
  1969 Addendum double page with Famous People and The Space Age
  1971 Addendum 4 pages Saga of Ships, Race Into Space, North American Wildlife in Danger etc.
4th Edition 1954 – 1972 (60 pages)
  1972 Addendum 2 pages with Animals and Their Young series and error card from Transportation Through the Ages
  1972 Addendum single page with History of Aviation
  1973 Addendum single page with The Arctic
  1973 Addendum 2 pages with Adventurers and Explorers and details of 7 reprinted series
5th Edition 1954 – 1975 (68 pages)
  1976 Addendum single page printed both sides with Wonders of Wildlife, Play Better Soccer
  1977 Addendum single page with Police File
  1978 Addendum 4 pages with Wonders of Wildlife, Play Better Soccer, Police File and Vanishing Wildlife
  1979 Addendum single page with Olympic Greats
  1980 Addendum single page printed both sides with Olympic Greats, Woodland Wildlife
6th Edition 1954 – 1981 (72 pages)
  1981 Addendum single page with Small Wonders details
  1983 Addendum single page printed both sides with Small Wonders, Queen Elizabeth I – Queen Elizabeth II
7th Edition 1954 – 1984 (84 pages)
  1985 Addendum single page with Incredible Creatures details

ISSUES OF IRELAND

Incredible Creatures. Size 69 x 37mm coloured numbered series of 40 issued in 1986 backs printed in green
Note: Backs printed in brown: see Issues of Great Britain

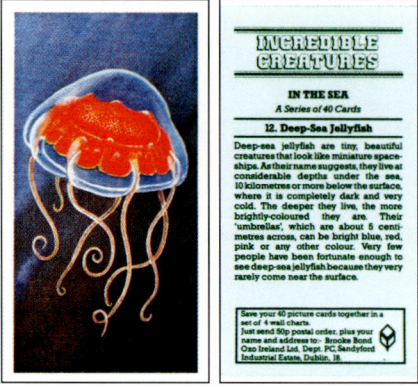

Miscellaneous Issues

Catch A Spy! Size 76 x 51mm coloured numbered series of 7 plus unnumbered certificate card. (Brooke Bond Secret Agent PG Tips Tea on one side and This is to certify that…… on the other). Issued 1977 backs printed in black. Leaflet issued advertising Catch A Spy Super Spy Book. The book has 24 pages and is inscribed on front cover "Catch A Spy! Brooke Bond Super Spy Book Full of Secrets & Games"
    1) Yuri Teaumov
    2) Brooke Bond
    3) Tyna Leaf
    4) Harry T, Strainer
    5) P. G. O'Trea
    6) Olga Teabagski
    7) Annie Teatime

Advertisement Cards and Inserts

PG Tips Token How to obtain free pens. Size 69 x37mm. Printed in black and white on yellow background. Issued around 1975.

ISSUES OF CANADA & U S A

African Animals. Size 69 x 37mm with rounded corners. Coloured numbered series of 48 inscribed "Series No. 7" with bilingual text in English and French. Backs printed in black and red. Issued in 1964 in Canada only. Special album issued with insert order form. Wallchart not seen.

Animals and Their Young. Size 69 x 37mm with rounded corners. Coloured numbered series of 48 inscribed "Series No. 15" with bilingual text in English and French. Backs printed in black and red Issued in 1972. Special album issued (No insert issued). Wallchart issued.
There are two printings of this set
    A) Canadian issues with Montreal address and black and red text on back
        1) Back with text ending with word products
        2) Back with text ending with words Tea/Coffee
Note: This series was also issued by Liptons Tea in Canada with Red Rose products on back.

Animals of North America. Size 69 x 37mm with rounded corners. Coloured numbered series of 48 inscribed "Series No. 2". Issued in 1960. Special album issued with insert order form. Wallchart issued.
There are five printings of this set
    A) Canadian issues with Montreal address and black text on back
        1) Rolland spelt with two L's
        2) Roland spelt with one L. 49mm between the two black blocks
        3) Roland spelt with one L. 47mm between the two black blocks
    B) U S A issues with New York address
        1) Black text on back
        2) Blue text on back

The Arctic. Size 69 x 37mm with rounded corners. Coloured numbered series of 48 inscribed "Series No. 16" with bilingual text in English and French. Backs printed in black and red Issued in 1973 in Canada only. Special album issued (No insert issued). Wallchart issued but only has 20 cards depicted
Two printings of card number 9 and 18
    No 9 A) Words on front of card "Hudson's Bay Company" white on black
            B) Words on front of card "Hudson's Bay Company" white on blue
    No 18 A) Text on eighth line with "Sir"
            B) Text on eighth line without "Sir"

Birds of North America. Size 69 x 37mm with rounded corners. Coloured numbered series of 48 inscribed "Series No. 4". Issued in 1962. Special album issued with insert order form. Wallchart issued.
There are three printings of this set
    A) Canadian issues with Montreal address and black and red text on back
        1) Thick card
        2) Paper thin card
    B) U S A issue with New York address and blue and black text on back

Butterflies of North America. Size 69 x 37mm with rounded corners. Coloured numbered series of 48 inscribed "Series No. 8" " with bilingual text in English and French. Issued in 1965. Special album issued (No insert issued). Wallchart issued.
There are two printings of this set
    A) Canadian issue with Montreal address and black and red text on back
    B) U S A issue with New York address and blue and red text on back

Canadian/American Songbirds. Size 69 x 37mm with rounded corners. Coloured numbered series of 48 inscribed "Series No. 9" with bilingual text in English and French. Issued in 1966. Special album issued (No insert issued). Wallchart issued.
There are two printings of this set
    A) Canadian issue with Montreal address and black and red text on back
    B) U S A issue with New York address and blue and red text on back

Dinosaurs. Size 69 x 37mm with rounded corners. Coloured numbered series of 48 inscribed "Series No. 5". Issued in 1963. Special album issued with insert order form. Wallchart issued but only has 18 cards depicted
There are two printings of this set
    A) Canadian issue with Montreal address and black and red text on back
    B) U S A issue with New York address and blue and black text on back

Exploring the Ocean. Size 69 x 37mm with rounded corners. Coloured numbered series of 48 inscribed "Series No. 14" with bilingual text in English and French. Backs printed in black and red. Issued in 1971 in Canada only. Special album issued. (No insert issued). Wallchart issued.

Indians of Canada. Size 69 x 37mm with rounded corners. Coloured numbered series of 48 inscribed "Series No. 17" with bilingual text in English and French. Backs printed in black and red. Issued in 1974 in Canada only. Special album issued. (No insert issued).Wallchart not seen.

North American Wildlife in Danger. Size 69 x 37mm with rounded corners. Coloured numbered series of 48 inscribed "Series No. 13" with bilingual text in English and French. Backs printed in black and red. Issued in 1970 in Canada only. Special album issued. (No insert issued). Wallchart not seen.

Songbirds of North America. Size 69 x 37mm with rounded corners. Coloured numbered series of 48 issued in 1959 in Canada only. Wallchart issued.
There are three printings of this set with Montreal address and black text on back
    A) Back "Red Rose Tea and Coffee" album clause reading
        1) Mount Your Collection, Send 25c
        2) Album available at your grocer's or from us 25c
    B) Back "Red Rose and Blue Ribbon Tea and Coffee"
Special album issued with two printings (No insert issued).
    A) Outside back cover words "Red Rose" only
    B) Outside back cover words "Red Rose & Blue Ribbon"

The Space Age. Size 69 x 37mm with rounded corners. Coloured numbered series of 48 inscribed "Series No. 12" with bilingual text in English and French. Backs printed in black and red. Issued in 1969 in Canada. Special album issued. (No insert issued). Wallchart issued.
Note the identical set was also issued in the USA

Transportation Through the Ages. Size 69 x 37mm with rounded corners. Coloured numbered series of 48 inscribed "Series No. 10" with bilingual text in English and French. Backs printed in black and red Issued in 1967 in Canada. Special album issued. (No insert issued). Wallchart issued.
Note the identical set was also issued in the USA
There are two printings of this set
   With Montreal address and black and red text on back
     A) Back with top line of text in red
     B) Back with top line of text in black
   There are two printings of card number 29 with top line in black text
     A) Red Rose advert on Bus on a pale blue background
     B) Red Rose advert on Bus on a white background

Trees of North America. Size 69 x 37mm with rounded corners. Coloured numbered series of 48 inscribed "Series No. 11" with bilingual text in English and French. Backs printed in black and red. Issued in 1968 in Canada. Wallchart issued.
Note the identical set was also issued in the USA
Special album issued with two printings (No insert issued).
   1) Background page colour green on pages 3,8,9,12,13,16,17,22 the rest in yellow
   2) Background page colour green on pages 3, 6,7,10,11,14,15,18,19,22 the rest in yellow

Tropical Birds. Size 69 x 37mm with rounded corners. Coloured numbered series of 48 inscribed "Series No. 6". With bilingual text in English and French. Issued in 1964. Special album issued with insert order form. Wallchart issued.
There are three printings of this set
   A) Canadian issues with Montreal address and black and red text on back
     1) Back with top line of text in red
     2) Back with top line of text in black
   B) U S A issue with New York address and blue and red text on back

Wild Flowers of North America. Size 69 x 37mm with rounded corners. Coloured numbered series of 48 inscribed "Series No. 3". Issued in 1961. Special album issued with insert order form. Wallchart issued
There are four printings of this set
   A) Canadian issue with Montreal address and black and red text on back
   B) U S A issues with New York address
     1) Dark blue and black text on back. Album price 25c with line through c slanting to the right
     2) Light blue and black text on back. Album price 25c with line through c slanting to the right
     3) Turquoise blue and black text on back. Album price 25c with line through c vertical, not slanting

No 31 — Series 7 Série — Set of/de 48
AFRICAN ANIMALS — ANIMAUX AFRICAINS

Diceros bicornis

BLACK RHINOCEROS The rhino, a relic of the past, is in grave danger of disappearing from the African scene. The large numbers that once browsed the thorn scrub have been reduced to a remnant not only by hunters but also by poachers who value their horns. Inasmuch as rhinos act as bulldozers, diligently rooting out the thorn sprouts, they make more room for grass, so important to the grazing animals. Without them the land goes back to brush.
ALBUMS AT MOST GROCERS—OR FROM US 25¢

Le RHINOCÉROS BICORNE d'Afrique
Le rhinocéros est malheureusement menacé d'extinction. Le nez de cet étrange animal porte deux cornes: celle de devant, pointue et très longue, celle de derrière, courte. La chasse de ce mastodonte offre de grands dangers car, blessé, il devient furieux, il s'élance avec la rapidité d'un cheval, bondit, renverse et foule aux pieds tout ce qu'il rencontre sur son passage.
ALBUMS CHEZ VOTRE ÉPICIER OU DIRECTEMENT—25¢

BROOKE BOND CANADA LIMITED
RED ROSE — BLUE RIBBON
Tea/Coffee Thé/Café

No 35 — Series 15 Série — Set of/de 48
ANIMALS AND THEIR YOUNG
LE JEUNE ANIMAL ET LES SIENS

Loxodonta africana

AFRICAN ELEPHANT A baby elephant lacks the ivory tusks of its parents; it will grow them eventually, but it possesses the elongated trunk, a useful bit of anatomy which is really a very long nose or proboscis that may be used in lieu of a hand. Baby elephants seem to have fun as they travel with the herd, running on their stubby legs to keep up and sometimes even chasing the attendant cattle egrets (birds) just for the fun of it.
SAVE YOUR CARDS IN AN ALBUM—ONLY 25¢

ÉLÉPHANT D'AFRIQUE L'éléphanteau ne possède pas de défenses. Il en obtiendra avec l'âge. Par contre, la nature l'a doté d'une trompe, organe souple et préhensile (il saisit) qui représente la lèvre supérieure. Le petit semble s'amuser en voyageant avec la troupe. Pour suivre, il est parfois obligé de courir, ce qui fait aussi pour le simple plaisir de pourchasser les aigrettes (oiseaux) qui accompagnent ces bêtes dans leurs déplacements.
CONSERVEZ VOS CARTES DANS UN ALBUM—25¢

BROOKE BOND FOODS LIMITED
5415 Côte de Liesse, Montréal 378, P.Q.
RED ROSE — BLUE RIBBON

No 41 — Series 15 Série — Set of/de 48
ANIMALS AND THEIR YOUNG
LE JEUNE ANIMAL ET LES SIENS

Odocoileus virginianus

WHITE-TAILED DEER A young fawn with its spotted coat and out-sized ears is a delightful little animal, wobbly on its slender legs at first, but soon able to keep up with its fast-moving mother. Three to five pounds at birth, it travels very little for a while, resting among the ferns and bushes until its foraging mother returns to nurse it. A fawn may be a single or it may have one brother or sister or rarely two.
SAVE YOUR CARDS IN AN ALBUM—ONLY 25¢

CERF DE VIRGINIE Le petit du cerf s'appelle faon et constitue l'un des animaux les plus séduisants. À sa naissance, très vacillant sur ses grêles jambes, il peut en peu de temps suivre sa mère qui se déplace très rapidement. Il pèse de 3 à 5 livres à la naissance et se déplace très peu pendant les premiers jours de sa vie. Il passe plutôt son temps dans un refuge garni de branchettes et de fougères où sa maman vient l'allaiter. Le cerf est un ruminant dont la femelle porte le nom de biche.
CONSERVEZ VOS CARTES DANS UN ALBUM—25¢

BROOKE BOND FOODS LIMITED
5415 Côte de Liesse, Montréal 378, P.Q.
RED ROSE — BLUE RIBBON
Tea/Coffee Thé/Café

No. 19 — Series No. 2 — Set of 48
ANIMALS OF NORTH AMERICA
Text by Roger Tory Peterson
Painted by Bob Hines

Castor canadensis
BEAVER
Le castor du Canada

The Beaver's fur, once used in making hats, sparked the conquest of the West. Trappers were ahead of most explorers. But as an upstream engineer each Beaver is worth many times the price of its pelt. Their dams slow up streams near the source, thereby controlling floods.

Conservez votre collection dans un album dont les textes sont de Roland Dumais—seulement 25¢
SAVE YOUR CARDS IN AN ALBUM!
AVAILABLE AT MOST GROCERS—OR FROM US 25¢

Cards are enclosed in packages of
RED ROSE AND BLUE RIBBON
TEA AND COFFEE

BROOKE BOND CANADA LIMITED
6201 Park Avenue, Montreal 8, P.Q.

No. 19 — Series No. 2 — Set of 48
ANIMALS OF NORTH AMERICA
Text by Roger Tory Peterson
Painted by Bob Hines

Castor canadensis
BEAVER
Le castor du Canada

The Beaver's fur, once used in making hats, sparked the conquest of the West. Trappers were ahead of most explorers. But as an upstream engineer each Beaver is worth many times the price of its pelt. Their dams slow up streams near the source, thereby controlling floods.

Conservez votre collection dans un album dont les textes sont de Roland Dumais—seulement 25¢
SAVE YOUR CARDS IN AN ALBUM!
AVAILABLE AT MOST GROCERS—OR FROM US 25¢

Cards are enclosed in packages of
RED ROSE AND BLUE RIBBON
TEA AND COFFEE

BROOKE BOND CANADA LIMITED
6201 Park Avenue, Montreal 8, P.Q.

No. 35 — Series No. 2 — Set of 48
ANIMALS OF NORTH AMERICA
Text by Roger Tory Peterson
Painted by Al Kreml

Odocoileus virginianus
WHITETAIL DEER
Le cerf de Virginie   (Le chevreuil)

In our rambles through the woods we sometimes surprise a deer which bounds away, flashing its white "flag." Dusk is the best time to see deer; they come into the open, munching a twig here, a leaf there. The millions of deer in North America today exceed the number in primeval times.

Conservez votre collection dans un album dont les textes sont de Roland Dumais—seulement 25¢
SAVE YOUR CARDS IN AN ALBUM!
AVAILABLE AT MOST GROCERS—OR FROM US 25¢

Cards are enclosed in packages of
RED ROSE TEA

BROOKE BOND TEA CO., Inc.
37 Old Slip, New York 5, N.Y.

No. 35 — Series No. 2 — Set of 48
ANIMALS OF NORTH AMERICA
Text by Roger Tory Peterson
Painted by Al Kreml

Odocoileus virginianus
WHITETAIL DEER
Le cerf de Virginie   (Le chevreuil)

In our rambles through the woods we sometimes surprise a deer which bounds away, flashing its white "flag." Dusk is the best time to see deer; they come into the open, munching a twig here, a leaf there. The millions of deer in North America today exceed the number in primeval times.

Conservez votre collection dans un album dont les textes sont de Roland Dumais—seulement 25¢
SAVE YOUR CARDS IN AN ALBUM!
AVAILABLE AT MOST GROCERS—OR FROM US 25¢

Cards are enclosed in packages of
RED ROSE TEA

BROOKE BOND TEA CO., Inc.
37 Old Slip, New York 5, N.Y.

THE ARCTIC — L'ARCTIQUE

No 32 Series 16 Série Set of/de 48

Ursus horribilis

GRIZZLY The high western mountains and the tundra of western Canada and Alaska are the native heath of this huge land carnivore which may weigh as much as half a ton. Its "dished-in" face, humped shoulders, and long claws distinguish it from other bears. Where it comes into contact with man, the grizzly loses out, but fortunately there are still great areas in the Arctic northwest where these shaggy giants can roam unmolested, travelling day or night in their never-ending search for food.
SAVE YOUR CARDS IN AN ALBUM—ONLY 25¢

GRIZZLY Les monts élevés et la toundra de l'Ouest canadien de même que l'Alaska constituent l'habitat de cet imposant carnivore (son poids peut atteindre 1000 lbs.). Son museau, sa bosse et ses longues griffes le distinguent des autres ours. Le grizzly doit combattre un humain arme est perdu d'avance naturellement. Toutefois, de vastes espaces libres existent encore dans le Nord-Ouest arctique où ce géant peut se promener en paix à la recherche de sa nourriture.
CONSERVEZ VOS CARTES DANS UN ALBUM—25¢

BROOKE BOND FOODS LIMITED
5415 Côte de Liesse, Montreal 378, P.Q.

Picture cards free in / Cartes gratuites dans le
The RED ROSE Tea

BIRDS OF NORTH AMERICA
Text by Roger Tory Peterson
Painted by Francis Lee Jaques

No. 41 Series No. 4 Set of 48

Larus argentatus
HERRING GULL
Goéland argenté

This big gull with black wing tips is the best known gull over much of North America. Actually it has had a population explosion in recent years. Whereas we were worried about its survival sixty years ago, it has increased tremendously since then. This is due partly to protection and also because garbage dumps, sewage beds and other sources of food aid their winter survival. Like most other birds of the sea the herring gull is able to drink salt water due to special glands.

Conservez votre collection dans un album dont les textes sont de Rolland Dumais — seulement 25¢ chez votre épicier ou écrivez-nous directement.
ALBUMS AT MOST GROCERS — OR FROM US 25¢
Cards free with RED ROSE and
BLUE RIBBON TEA and COFFEE
BROOKE BOND CANADA LIMITED
4305 Côte de Liesse, Montreal 9, P.Q.

BIRDS OF NORTH AMERICA
Text by Roger Tory Peterson
Painted by Walter A. Weber

No. 13 Series No. 4 Set of 48

Anas discors
BLUE-WINGED TEAL
Sarcelle à ailes bleues

Among the marsh ducks that puddle and tip up, there are often little half-sized fellows. When they fly some may show large pale blue patches on the forewing. These are likely to be blue-winged teal (although in the far west they might prove to be cinnamon teal). A white crescent on the face of the male is another good mark. The blue-wing breeds as far north as Great Slave Lake in Canada and may travel as far as northern South America in the winter.

Conservez votre collection dans un album dont les textes sont de Rolland Dumais — seulement 25¢ chez votre épicier ou écrivez-nous directement.
ALBUMS AT MOST GROCERS — OR FROM US 25¢
Cards are enclosed in packages of
RED ROSE TEA AND COFFEE
BROOKE BOND TEA CO., Inc.
37 Old Slip, New York 5, N. Y.

BUTTERFLIES OF PAPILLONS DE
NORTH AMERICA L'AMÉRIQUE DU NORD

No 42 Series 8 Série Set of/de 48

Colias eurytheme
ALFALFA BUTTERFLY The "Orange Sulphur," as it is often called, seems to hybridize freely with the Common Sulphur, producing butterflies that are yellow with a flush of orange. Within the past forty years the orange sulphur, a more southern and midwestern butterfly, has extended its range northeastward through New York and New England to the mountain provinces of Canada. Whereas the caterpillars of the Common Sulphur prefer clover those of the Orange Sulphur favour alfalfa. Both gather at roadside puddles.
SAVE YOUR CARDS IN AN ALBUM — ONLY 25¢

COLIADE DE LA LUZERNE. Il se produit souvent des croisements entre ce lépidoptère et le coliade du trèfle. Il en résulte des spécimens dont la teinte est d'un orangé clair. Depuis une quarantaine d'années, le territoire du coliade de la luzerne s'étire de plus en plus vers le Nord-Est et couvre une bonne partie du Canada. Tel que son nom le suggère, ce coliade, à l'état de chenille, se nourrit surtout de luzerne.
CONSERVEZ VOS CARTES DANS UN ALBUM—25¢

BROOKE BOND CANADA LIMITED
4305 Côte de Liesse, Montreal 9, P.Q.

Cards free in RED ROSE — BLUE RIBBON
Cartes gratuites dans Tea/Coffee Thé/Café

BUTTERFLIES OF PAPILLONS DE
NORTH AMERICA L'AMÉRIQUE DU NORD

No 2 Series 8 Série Set of/de 48

Euptychia cymela
LITTLE WOOD SATYR This modest little butterfly flits through the open woods, staying close to the grass and trees, disappearing into the shadows and reappearing a few feet away. Small wet meadows spotted with bushes and surrounded by woods are a favourite resort. Like the caterpillars of other "satyrs" and "wood nymphs," its caterpillar feeds on grasses. It ranges from southern Canada to the Gulf of Mexico.
SAVE YOUR CARDS IN AN ALBUM — ONLY 25¢

"PETIT SATYRE DES BOIS" Ce satyre vit et se promène dans les éclaircies. Son vol bas l'oblige à contourner branches et brindilles. Sitôt est-il apparu qu'il disparaît derrière un arbre ou le feuillage d'une plante quelconque. Comme la chenille des autres satyres, la sienne est herbivore et vit de la nourriture que lui offrent les plantes herbeuses. Ce satyre est répandu depuis le Sud du Canada jusqu'au Golfe du Mexique. Dans notre pays, on le voit rarement avant la fin de mai.
CONSERVEZ VOS CARTES DANS UN ALBUM—25¢

BROOKE BOND TEA CO., Inc.
37 Old Slip, New York, N. Y. 10005

Cards are enclosed in packages of
Brooke Bond/RED ROSE Tea

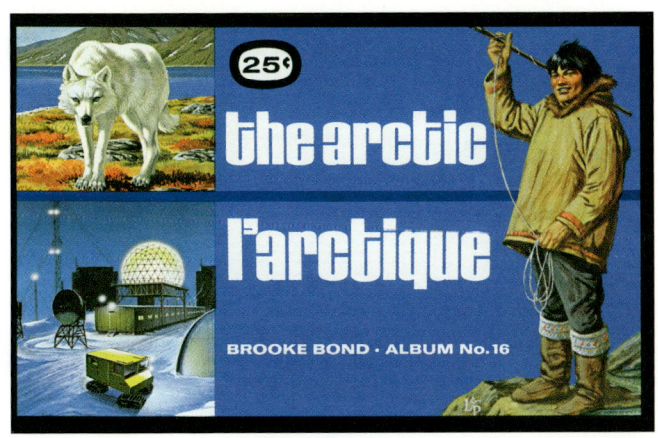

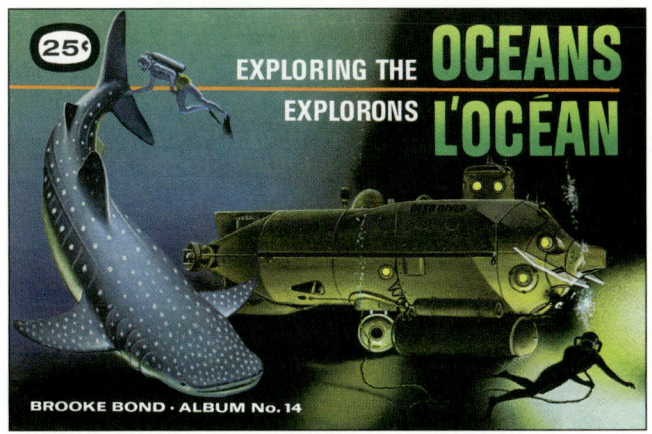

No 29   Series 17 Série   Set of/de 48

INDIANS OF CANADA—LES INDIENS DU CANADA

SIGN LANGUAGE *(Plains)* The Indian was eloquent in speech, with an oral literature rich in legends, songs and prayers. Canadian Indians had eleven unrelated language groups, broken into many more dialects. Yet many could communicate by a logical and easily understood sign language. This was best developed on the plains where wandering tribes speaking different tongues often met in alliance or council. The sign shown means *tipi* or lodge.

SAVE YOUR CARDS IN AN ALBUM—ONLY 25¢

LANGAGE PAR SIGNES *(Plaines)* L'Amérindien parlait avec éloquence et possédait une tradition orale riche en légendes, chants et prières. Les Amérindiens canadiens pouvaient se regrouper en 11 groupes linguistiques qui se fractionnaient en un grand nombre de dialectes. Malgré tout, plusieurs groupes pouvaient communiquer entre eux grâce à un langage par signes logique et facile à comprendre. Les indigènes qui erraient dans les plaines avaient perfectionné ce langage qui leur permettait de faire des alliances et de tenir des conseils. Le signe de l'image signifie "hutte".

CONSERVEZ VOS CARTES DANS UN ALBUM—25¢

BROOKE BOND FOODS LIMITED
5415 Côte de Liesse, Montreal H4P 1A3, P.Q.

Picture cards free in / Cartes gratuites dans le
Thé **RED ROSE** Tea

No 15   Series 13 Série   Set of/de 48

NORTH AMERICAN WILDLIFE IN DANGER
NOTRE FAUNE EN PERIL

Enhydra lutris

SEA OTTER Pursued from the Aleutians to California for its valuable fur, this marine animal was brought very close to extinction. Fortunately a few survived and under protection have increased, especially in the Aleutians where a strong population thrives around Amchitka. Sea otters may be seen most easily near the Monterey Peninsula of California where they float, belly up, amongst beds of kelp. Rediscovered in 1938, the California population may now be 500 to 600.

SAVE YOUR CARDS IN AN ALBUM—ONLY 25¢

LOUTRE DE MER Parée d'une magnifique fourrure, cette loutre a été victime d'une chasse intense dans les eaux se situant entre les Aléoutiennes et la Californie. Sur le bord de l'extinction il y a quelque temps, elle est maintenant, grâce à la protection dont elle jouit, en train de se répandre à nouveau dans les Aléoutiennes, à proximité d'Amchitka. La péninsule de Monterey, en Californie, abrite aussi des familles de loutres de mer redécouvertes en 1938 et comptant en tout entre 500 et 600 membres.

CONSERVEZ VOS CARTES DANS UN ALBUM—25¢

BROOKE BOND FOODS LIMITED
5415 Côte de Liesse, Montreal 378, P.Q.

Cards free with   **RED ROSE—BLUE RIBBON**
Cartes gratuites avec   Tea/Coffee   Thé/Café

No. 4 set of 48	No. 19 set of 48	No. 19 set of 48
SONGBIRDS OF NORTH AMERICA	**SONGBIRDS OF NORTH AMERICA**	**SONGBIRDS OF NORTH AMERICA**
Text by Roger Tory Peterson	*Text by Roger Tory Peterson*	*Text by Roger Tory Peterson*
Painted by Roger Tory Peterson	*Painted by Walter A. Weber*	*Painted by Walter A. Weber*
MAGNOLIA WARBLER	**BAY-BREASTED WARBLER**	**BAY-BREASTED WARBLER**
Fauvette à tête cendrée	Fauvette à poitrine baie	Fauvette à poitrine baie
In summer, the home of this black and yellow warbler with the flashing tail band is the fir belt of Canada, east of the Rockies. There at the edge of some opening in the evergreen forest, it builds its shallow cup of rootlets in a low spruce or hemlock. Eggs (4) are spotted. Length 5".	In spruce forests from Newfoundland to Alberta the Bay-breasted Warbler sings a high lisping song in early summer. Moulting in late summer into a drab greenish plumage, the birds soon depart for the tropics. The nest, a frail cup high in an evergreen, holds 5 speckled eggs. Length 5½".	In spruce forests from Newfoundland to Alberta the Bay-breasted Warbler sings a high lisping song in early summer. Moulting in late summer into a drab greenish plumage, the birds soon depart for the tropics. The nest, a frail cup high in an evergreen, holds 5 speckled eggs. Length 5½".
Conservez votre collection sur une carte murale avec descriptions. Seulement 25¢ Mount your collection. Send 25¢ for colorful wall chart.	Conservez votre collection dans un album en couleurs avec descriptions. Seulement 25¢ chez votre épicier, ou écrivez-nous directement. Albums available at your grocer's or from us—price 25¢.	Conservez votre collection dans un album en couleurs avec descriptions. Seulement 25¢ chez votre épicier, ou écrivez-nous directement. SAVE YOUR CARDS IN A COLORFUL ALBUM! AVAILABLE AT YOUR GROCER'S OR FROM US—25¢
Cards are enclosed in packages of RED ROSE TEA AND COFFEE	Cards are enclosed in packages of RED ROSE TEA AND COFFEE	Cards are enclosed in packages of RED ROSE AND BLUE RIBBON TEA AND COFFEE
BROOKE BOND CANADA LIMITED 6201 Park Avenue, Montreal 8, P. Q.	BROOKE BOND CANADA LIMITED 6201 Park Avenue, Montreal 8, P. Q.	BROOKE BOND CANADA LIMITED 6201 Park Avenue, Montreal 8, P. Q.

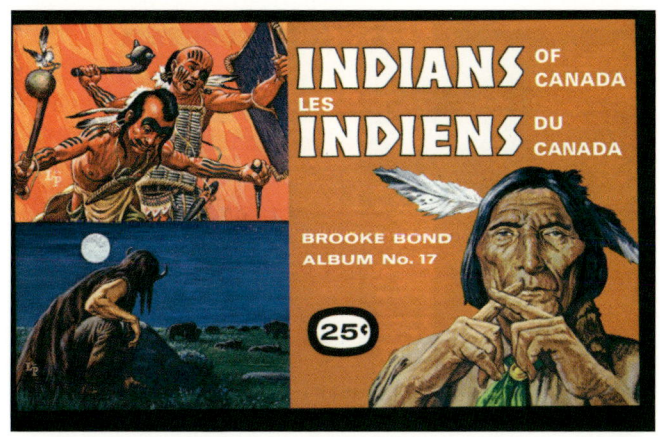

88

No 24 — Series 6 Série — Set of/de 48
TROPICAL BIRDS / OISEAUX TROPICAUX
Eumomota superciliosa

TURQUOISE-BROWED MOTMOT In tropical forests from Mexico to northern Argentina live eight species of motmots. The peculiar tails have two long central shafts with racketlike tips. Apparently the new feathers have vanes along the entire shaft but for several inches these are quite brittle and break off when the bird preens. Like kingfishers to which they are related, motmots sit in silent meditation on exposed branches and sally forth to catch the large insects that tempt them.

ALBUMS AT MOST GROCERS—OR FROM US 25¢

MOMOT À SOURCILS BLEUS Huit espèces de Momots vivent dans les forêts tropicales du Mexique jusqu'au nord de l'Argentine. Ces oiseaux se distinguent à leur queue qui se prolonge en deux hampes terminées par une houppette. Ces plumes sont pourvues de barbes qui tombent quand l'oiseau lisse son plumage. Apparenté au Martin-Pêcheur, le Momot demeure immobile et silencieux, sur une branche exposée, jusqu'à ce qu'il se laisse tenter par un gros insecte au vol.

ALBUMS CHEZ VOTRE ÉPICIER OU DIRECTEMENT—25¢

BROOKE BOND CANADA LIMITED
4305 Côte de Liesse, Montréal 9, P.Q.

Cards free with / Cartes gratuites avec — **RED ROSE — BLUE RIBBON Tea/Coffee Thé/Café**

No 24 — Series 6 Série — Set of/de 48
TROPICAL BIRDS / OISEAUX TROPICAUX
Eumomota superciliosa

TURQUOISE-BROWED MOTMOT In tropical forests from Mexico to northern Argentina live eight species of motmots. The peculiar tails have two long central shafts with racketlike tips. Apparently the new feathers have vanes along the entire shaft but for several inches these are quite brittle and break off when the bird preens. Like kingfishers to which they are related, motmots sit in silent meditation on exposed branches and sally forth to catch the large insects that tempt them.

ALBUMS AT MOST GROCERS—OR FROM US 25¢

MOMOT À SOURCILS BLEUS Huit espèces de Momots vivent dans les forêts tropicales du Mexique jusqu'au nord de l'Argentine. Ces oiseaux se distinguent à leur queue qui se prolonge en deux hampes terminées par une houppette. Ces plumes sont pourvues de barbes qui tombent quand l'oiseau lisse son plumage. Apparenté au Martin-Pêcheur, le Momot demeure immobile et silencieux, sur une branche exposée, jusqu'à ce qu'il se laisse tenter par un gros insecte au vol.

ALBUMS CHEZ VOTRE ÉPICIER OU DIRECTEMENT—25¢

BROOKE BOND CANADA LIMITED
4305 Côte de Liesse, Montréal 9, P.Q.

Cards free with / Cartes gratuites avec — **RED ROSE — BLUE RIBBON Tea/Coffee Thé/Café**

No 4 — Series 6 Série — Set of/de 48
TROPICAL BIRDS / OISEAUX TROPICAUX
Branta sandvicensis

NENE This goose once widespread in the Hawaiian Islands became scarce when ships brought increasing numbers of settlers. By 1950 there were very few nenes left in the world, perhaps less than 50, and most of these were in the Honolulu Zoo. Since then, both the Wildfowl Trust in England and the experts in Hawaii have raised many in captivity. There are now at least 400 and dozens are being returned yearly to their old haunts on the volcanic slopes of Hawaii and Maui.

SAVE YOUR CARDS IN AN ALBUM — ONLY 25¢

BERNACHE HAWAÏENNE Cette oie, très répandue un certain temps dans la région d'Hawaii disparut presque complètement à l'arrivée des premiers colonisateurs. Ces bernaches devinrent très rares, si bien qu'en 1950, on n'en comptait que quelques spécimens dans le monde. La plupart étaient gardées au jardin zoologique d'Honolulu. Depuis, grâce au travail des ornithologues, des Bernaches hawaïennes, élevées en captivité, sont relâchées tous les ans dans leurs anciens habitats.

CONSERVEZ VOS CARTES DANS UN ALBUM.—25¢

BROOKE BOND TEA CO., Inc.
37 Old Slip, New York, N.Y. 10005

Cards are enclosed in packages of **Brooke Bond / RED ROSE Tea**

No. 34 — Series No. 3 — Set of 48
WILD FLOWERS OF NORTH AMERICA
Text by Roger Tory Peterson
Painted by Don R. Eckelberry

Epilobium latifolium
BROAD-LEAVED WILLOW-HERB
L'épilobe à larges feuilles

This showy flower blooms during the summer months in moist ground in Alaska and across northern Canada to Newfoundland. The bright rose petals brighten the gray stony banks and bars of northern streams. Like the similar Fireweed it has four petals. It belongs to the evening primrose family.

OFFICIAL FLOWER OF THE YUKON

Conservez votre collection dans un album dont les textes sont de Rolland Dumais—seulement 25¢ chez votre épicier ou écrivez-nous directement.

SAVE YOUR CARDS IN AN ALBUM! AT MOST GROCERS'—OR FROM US. 25¢

Cards are enclosed in packages of **RED ROSE AND BLUE RIBBON TEA AND COFFEE**

BROOKE BOND CANADA LIMITED
4305 Côte de Liesse, Montréal 9, P.Q.

No. 4 — Series No. 3 — Set of 48
WILD FLOWERS OF NORTH AMERICA
Text by Roger Tory Peterson
Painted by Don R. Eckelberry

Lilium philadelphicum
WOOD-LILY
Le lis de Philadelphie

The Wood-Lily, which blossoms in July, is the most richly colored wild lily, running the gamut from orange to scarlet. The "six-petalled" flowers are erect, like a cup, not nodding and bell-like as are those of the Canada Lily. Wood edges and old pastures are the Wood-Lily's environment.

PROVINCIAL FLOWER OF SASKATCHEWAN

Conservez votre collection dans un album dont les textes sont de Rolland Dumais—seulement 25¢ chez votre épicier ou écrivez-nous directement.

SAVE YOUR CARDS IN AN ALBUM! AT MOST GROCERS'—OR FROM US. 25¢

Cards are enclosed in packages of **RED ROSE TEA**

BROOKE BOND TEA CO., Inc.
37 Old Slip, New York 5, N.Y.

Set Completion Cards Size 69 x 37mm
Single card issues with rounded corners. Identical issues in Canada and USA from series 1 to 12. Series 13 14 and 15 not issued in the USA.

Series 2	Animals of North America. Printed in brown issued in 1961
Series 3	Wild Flowers of North America. Printed in green issued in 1962
Series 4	Birds of North America. Printed in blue issued in 1963
Series 5	Dinosaurs. Printed in purple issued in 1964
Series 6	Tropical Birds. Printed in orange issued in 1965
Series 7	African Animals. Printed in black issued in 1965
Series 8	Butterflies of North America. Printed in brown issued in 1966
Series 9	Canadian/American Songbirds. Printed in blue issued in 1967
Series 10	Transportation Through the Ages. Printed in green issued in 1968
Series 11	Trees of North America. Printed in blue issued in 1969
Series 12	Space Age. Printed in purple issued in 1970
Series 13	North American Wildlife in Danger. Printed in blue issued in 1971
Series 14	Exploring the Oceans. Printed in black issued in 1972
Series 15	Animals and their Young. Printed in brown issued in 1973

Set Completion Cards Size 63 x 54mm

Series 1	Songbirds of North America. Printed in black issued in 1960
Series 2	Animals of North America. Printed in brown issued in 1961
Series 3	Wild Flowers of North America. Printed in green issued in 1962
Series 4	Birds of North America. Printed in blue issued in 1963
Series 7	African Animals. Printed in black issued in 1965
Series 8	Butterflies of North America. Printed in brown issued in 1966
Series 9	Canadian/American Songbirds. Printed in black issued in 1967
Series 10	Transportation Through the Ages. Printed in brown/dark red issued in 1968
Series 13	North American Wildlife in Danger. Printed in blue issued in 1971

Set Completion Cards Size 80 x 76mm (Printed on thick board)

Series 1	Songbirds of North America. Printed in black issued in 1960
Series 4	Birds of North America. Printed in blue issued in 1963
Series 8	Butterflies of North America. Printed in brown issued in 1966

Set Completion Leaflets

Type 1
Printed in colour with picture of album cover and tick boxes for ordering single cards. Size 134 x 78mm printed in English on one side and French on reverse. Identical issues in Canada and USA.

Series 2	Animals of North America album picture, single cards for Songbirds of North America
Series 3	Wild Flowers of North America album picture, single cards for Animals of North America
Series 4	Birds of North America album picture, single cards for Wild Flowers of North America
Series 5	Dinosaurs album picture, single cards for Birds of North America
Series 6	Tropical Birds album picture, single cards for Dinosaurs
Series 7	African Animals album picture, single cards for Tropical Birds.

Type 2
Text only no border with tick boxes for ordering single cards size 105 x 75mm

Canadian issues with Montreal address.

Series 6	Tropical Birds. Printed on white paper
Series 7	African Animals. Printed on white paper
Series 8	Butterflies of North America. Printed on buff paper
Series 9	Candian/American Songbirds. Printed on orange paper
Series 10	Transportation Through the Ages. Printed on dark yellow paper
Series 11	Trees of North America. Printed on blue green paper
Series 12	The Space Age. Printed on yellow paper
Series 13	North American Wildlife in Danger. Printed on pale blue paper
Series 14	Exploring the Oceans. Printed on pale green paper
Series 15	Animals and Their Young. Printed on pink paper
Series 16	The Arctic. Printed on pale mustard paper
Series 17	Indians of Canada. Printed on pale green paper (note size 165 x 75mm includes announcement stating "This is the last of the picture card series, ...)

USA issues with New York address.

Series 6	Tropical Birds. Printed on yellow paper (lists Butterfly album as African Animals series was not issued in the USA)
Series 8	Butterflies of North America. Printed on blue paper
Series 9	Canadian/American Songbirds. Printed on orange paper
Series 10	Transportation Through the Ages. Printed on dark yellow paper
Series 11	Trees of North America. Printed on blue green paper

Free Album Offer Leaflets
Type 1
Canada issues inscribed "Red Rose Tea and Blue Ribbon Coffee" (except series 16 and 17) underneath a picture of two cards on the right hand side and a black and white picture of the album cover on left hand side. Uncoloured Size 102 x 63mm. Without tick boxes for ordering single cards

Series 7   African Animals - yellow background
Series 8   Butterflies of North America – orange background
Series 9   Canadian/American Songbirds – red background
Series 10   Transportation Through The Ages – blue background
Series 11   Trees of North America – green background
Series 12   The Space Age – orange background
Series 13   North American Wildlife in Danger – green background
Series 14   Exploring the Oceans – blue background
Series 15   Animals and Their Young – green background
Series 16   The Arctic (Red Rose Tea only) – blue background
Series 17   Indians of Canada (Red Rose Tea only) – brown background

USA issues with Red Rose Tea only
Series 8   Butterflies of North America – orange background
Series 9   Canadian/American Songbirds – red background
Series 10   Transportation Through The Ages – blue background
Series 11   Trees of North America – green background
Series 12   The Space Age – orange background

Type 2
USA Issues. Text only with fancy border without tick boxes for ordering single cards plain back.
Series 4   Birds of North America black print on blue paper size 106 x 70mm
Series 5   Dinosaurs black print on yellow paper size 107 x 71mm
Series 6   Tropical Birds purple print on white paper size 110 x 71mm

Brooke Bond Naturalist Club Certificates
These certificates were obtained in exchange for sending in the completed form from inside the album. Printed in colour.
Series 2   Animals of North America
Series 3   Wild Flowers of North America
Series 4   Birds of North America
Series 5   Dinosaurs
Series 6   Tropical Birds

ISSUES OF SOUTHERN RHODESIA & EAST AFRICA

African Birds. Size 69 x 37mm coloured numbered series of 50 issued in 1965 backs printed in magenta. Special album issued price 50 cents.

African Wild Life. Size 69 x 37mm coloured numbered series of 50 issued in 1961 backs printed in green with Nairobi and Salisbury addresses. Special album issued front cover with no price and red line under "C. F. Tunnicliffe, R. A.", back also differs from Great Britain issue with no text underneath Brooke Bond in oval. Wallchart issued titled East African Wildlife.

Asian Wild Life. Size 69 x 37mm coloured numbered series of 50 issued in 1963 backs printed in magenta with Nairobi and Salisbury addresses. Special album issued front cover with price 50 cents in East Africa and 6d in Rhodesia.

Bird Portraits This set and album was issued in 1960 and are identical to the Great Britain issue.

Butterflies of the World. Size 69 x 37mm coloured numbered series of 50 issued in 1966 backs printed in magenta. Special album issued cover with price 9d (Note Great Britain issue 6d).

Tropical Birds. Size 69 x 37mm coloured numbered series of 50 issued in 1962 backs printed in magenta with Nairobi and Salisbury addresses. Special album issued front cover with no price and red line under "C. F. Tunnicliffe, R. A.", back also differs from Great Britain issue with no text underneath Brooke Bond in oval.

Wildlife in Danger. Size 69 x 37mm coloured numbered series of 50 issued in 1964 backs printed in magenta. Special album issued front cover with "Price 50 cents" printed on bottom right corner in East Africa and "PRICE NINEPENCE" in Rhodesia. (Note Great Britain issue 6d)

Set Completion Cards
Single card issues size 69 x 37mm
African Wild Life. Printed in black issued in 1962

Note Wallcharts were issued for East African Birds 1st series and East African Birds 2nd series but no sets of cards were issued.

A SERIES OF 50. No. 15
AFRICAN BIRDS
Illustrated by C. F. Tunnicliffe, R.A. and described by John G. Williams

VULTURINE GUINEA-FOWL
(Acryllium vulturinum)

This guinea-fowl earned its name by the naked resemblance its small cranium and heavy bill bear to the head of a vulture. The effect is further enhanced by a nape ruff of soft velvety feathers. But there the likeness ends. The Vulturine Guinea-fowl is one of the most outstanding African game birds. Outside the nesting season the birds gather into large companies, sometimes a hundred or more strong. The sight of these birds travelling en masse through semi-desert bush country to some favoured water-hole is something no naturalist can ever forget. The species has a somewhat restricted distribution from Somaliland to north-eastern Tanganyika. Length twenty-four inches.

GET A PICTURE CARD ALBUM FROM YOUR GROCER
Issued for Educational purposes by
BROOKE BOND

A SERIES OF 50. No. 38
AFRICAN WILD LIFE
Illustrated and described by C. F. Tunnicliffe, R.A.

ORYX
(Oryx beisa annectens)

There are several species of oryx in Africa, the one depicted being the Beisa Oryx of East Africa. It is an animal of the dry bush and the semi-desert country. Oryx live in herds. Both sexes are horned, the males being quarrelsome and often indulging in fierce fights. The females have longer, thinner horns than the males, but in both they are very deadly weapons, especially against dogs, which poaching natives employ to hunt the oryx. Probably as a protection the skin on their necks and shoulders is nearly an inch thick.

GET A PICTURE CARD ALBUM FROM YOUR GROCER
Issued by
BROOKE BOND
P.O. Box 1160, Nairobi
P.O. Box 6, Southerton, Salisbury, S.R.

A SERIES OF 50. No. 33
ASIAN WILD LIFE
Illustrated and described by C. F. Tunnicliffe, R.A.

BLACKBUCK
(Antilope cervicapra)

In India, from the northern plains to Cape Comorin, the Blackbuck may be found where the country is suitable—grassy districts or cultivated areas being its choice. It wanders about in herds of from 10 to 50, though it has, at times, been observed in hundreds. Only the males have the long spiral horns, and only fully adult males have the black-brown and white coat. Young males and all females are yellowish-fawn and white. Blackbuck are immensely fast and have great stamina. Few animals can overtake them on good ground. The males are quarrelsome in the rutting season and fight much among themselves.

GET A PICTURE CARD ALBUM FROM YOUR GROCER
Issued by
BROOKE BOND
P.O. Box 2011, Nairobi
P.O. Box 6, Southerton, Salisbury, S.R.

A SERIES OF 50. No. 12
BUTTERFLIES OF THE WORLD
Illustrated and described by Richard Ward

Kallima inachus
NYMPHALIDAE
(Orange Oakleaf)

It is said that the undersides of these Leaf Butterflies, when at rest with wings closed, are indistinguishable from leaves. The colour and type of pattern of the undersides are known as 'Protective Resemblance.' These butterflies are on the wing during the rainy season and have a liking for flowering trees and bushes. K. inachus ranges through India, Kashmir, Burma West and South China. Wingspan approx. 3½ inches.

GET A PICTURE CARD ALBUM FROM YOUR GROCER
Issued for Educational purposes by
BROOKE BOND

A SERIES OF 50. No. 23
TROPICAL BIRDS
Illustrated and described by C. F. Tunnicliffe, R.A.

SCARLET MACAW
(Ara macao)

Sometimes known as Red-and-Yellow Macaw, this gorgeous parrot, familiar as a pet, is mainly found in the tropical forests of America, where it moves in flocks through the high trees, feeding on fruit, and filling the forest with harsh calls. They feed during the first hours of daylight, then, after drinking and bathing, they retire to deep shade when the sun is high. In the afternoon they feed again, and before they roost all gather in a large tree. They nest in the hollows of trees, and sometimes the nest is betrayed by the protruding tail of the sitting bird. Usually two eggs are laid. Length of adult about 39 inches.

GET A PICTURE CARD ALBUM FROM YOUR GROCER
Issued by
BROOKE BOND
P.O. Box 2011, Nairobi
P.O. Box 6, Southerton, Salisbury, S.R.

A SERIES OF 50. No. 5
WILDLIFE IN DANGER
Illustrated and described by Peter Scott

INDRI
(Indri indri)

Once described as the 'dog-faced man,' this large tail-less Lemur lives in the indigenous forests of Madagascar where it is called Babakoto. It is marvellously acrobatic in the high trees and has a loud cry which almost amounts to a song. Its native forests have been greatly reduced so that there are only two places where the Indri can still be found. The main danger lies in the continued destruction of the forests. One reserve has recently been established for them and it is hoped that other areas will also be set aside.

GET A PICTURE CARD ALBUM FROM YOUR GROCER
Issued for Educational purposes by
BROOKE BOND

ISSUES OF SOUTH AFRICA

African Wild Life/Wild Van Afrika. Size 69 x 37mm. Coloured number series of 50 issued in 1965. Backs printed in blue with alternate Afrikaans and English text with Pretoria address. Odd numbers have English text and even numbers have Afrikaans text.

 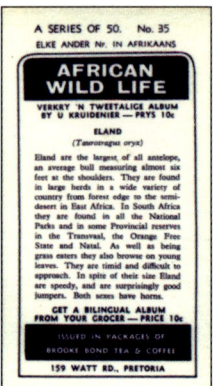 

African Wild Life/Wild Van Afrika. Size 69 x 37mm. Coloured number series of 50 issued in 1965. Backs printed in blue with bilingual Afrikaans and English text with Pretoria address. Special album issued with bilingual text.

Our Pets. Size 69 x 37mm. Coloured number series of 50 issued in 1967. Backs printed in blue with bilingual Afrikaans and English text with Pretoria address. Special album issued for printing A with insert order form.
There are 2 printings of this set with the first 14 cards being exactly the same in each printing.

Printing A
1. The Alsation
2. The Beagle
3. The Boxer
4. The Fox Terrier
5. The Ridgeback
6. The Poodle
7. The Cairn Terrier
8. The Siamese Cat
9. The Tabby Cat
10. The Persian Cat
11. A Vivarium
12. Goldfish
13. Exotic Fish
14. The Donkey
15. The Shetland Pony
16. The Boerperd
17. Ponies
18. The Guinea Pig
19. The White Rat
20. Mice
21. The Rabbit

Printing B (Rarer printing)
1. The Alsation
2. The Beagle
3. The Boxer
4. The Fox Terrier
5. The Ridgeback
6. The Poodle
7. The Cairn Terrier
8. The Siamese Cat
9. The Tabby Cat
10. The Persian Cat
11. A Vivarium
12. Goldfish
13. Exotic Fish
14. The Donkey
15. The Marmoset
16. The Vervet Monkey
17. The Nagapie
18. The House Snake
19. The Mole Snake
20. The Angora Goat
21. The Goose

22. The Hamster	22. The Duck
23. The Angora Rabbit	23. The Rabbit
24. The Goose	24. The Angora Rabbit
25. The Duck	25. Bees
26. The Blue Crane	26. The White Rat
27. The Peafowl	27. Mice
28. The Macaw	28. The Canary
29. The Cockatoo	29. The Blue Crane
30. The Fantail Pigeon	30. The Peafowl
31. The Canary	31. The Silkworm
32. The East African Grey Parrot	32. The Lamb
33. The Crow	33. The Homing or Racing Pigeon
34. The Homing or Racing Pigeon	34. The Fantail Pigeon
35. The Budgerigar	35. The Guinea Pig
36. The Java Sparrow	36. The Hedgehog
37. The Nagapie	37. The Crow
38. The Marmoset	38. The East African Grey Parrot
39. The Vervet Monkey	39. The Macaw
40. Bees	40. The Cockatoo
41. The Lamb	41. The Budgerigar
42. The Terrapin	42. The Java Sparrow
43. The Chameleon	43. The Shetland Pony
44. The Silkworm	44. Ponies
45. The Duiker	45. The Boerperd
46. The Angora Goat	46. The Hamster
47. The Tortoise	47. The Duiker
48. The Hedgehog	48. The Terrapin
49. The House Snake	49. The Tortoise
50. The Mole Snake	50. The Chameleon

Out Into Space. Size 69 x 37mm. Coloured numbered series of 50 issued in 1966. Backs printed in blue with bilingual Afrikaans and English text with Pretoria address. Special album issued with price 10c.

Set Completion Cards
Single card issues size 68 x 37mm

African Wild Life. Printed in black issued in 1966

Our Pets. Printed in black issued in 1968

ISSUES OF MUSGRAVE-BROOKE BOND IRELAND

British Birds by Frances Pitt. Size 69 x 37mm coloured numbered series of 20 issued in 1964 backs printed in blue with Musgrave Brothers Ltd Cork address. Special album issued price 6d..

British Wild Life. Size 69 x 37mm coloured numbered series of 50 issued in 1964 backs printed in blue with Musgrave Brothers Ltd. Cork address. Special album issued with Musgrave Brothers Ltd on back.

Butterflies of the World. Size 69 x 37mm coloured numbered series of 50 issued in 1965 backs printed in magenta with Musgrave-Brooke Bond Cork address. Special album issued with cover price 6d.

Transport Through The Ages. Size 69 x 37mm coloured numbered series of 50 issued in 1966 backs printed in magenta with Musgrave-Brooke Bond Cork address Special album issued with Musgrave printed on front top right hand side of cover

 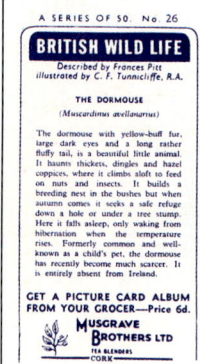 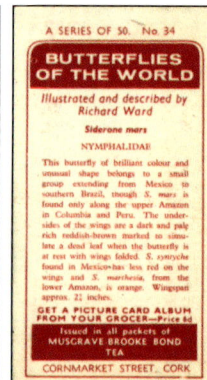 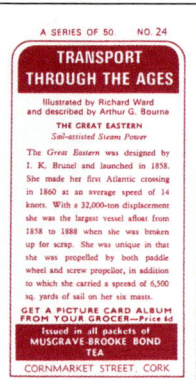

Miscellaneous – Advertisement cards and Inserts
Matchmaker Gift Cards.
Size 68 x 37mm. Issued in 1967. Each card has a right or left hand picture of a gift, if both halves were collected they could be exchanged for the gift they depicted.
Three printings of this series as follows:
    A) Printed in blue and black with Musgrave Brooke Bond printed on front
    B) Printed in blue and black with P G Tips printed on front
    C) Printed in red and black
There is also an announcement card saying "The Matchmaker Gift Scheme will soon finish" etc

Printing A and B: 39 different gifts. All left hand pictures are known and only 1 right hand picture number 25 in printing A has been seen. Left hand halves being the common issue.

1. 12 Piece Tea Service
2. 21 Piece Tea Service
3. Bathroom Scales
4. Battery Operated Clock
5. Children's Cutlery Set
6. Chip Pan & Basket
7. Electric Blanket
8. Electric Cooker
9. Electric Fire
10. Electric Kettle
11. Electric Toaster
12. Fan Heater
13. Floor Mop
14. Folding Deck Chair
15. Food Mixer
16. Football
17. Fridge
18. Hair Dryer
19. Ironing Board
20. Kitchen Scales
21. Lawn Mower
22. Non-Stick Frying Pan
23. Paint Box
24. Pencil Set
25. Pillow Cases
26. Pressure Cooker
27. Sheets
28. Souvenir Tea Cloths
29. Steam Iron
30. Tea Caddy
31. Tea Pot
32. Teddy Bear
33. Top Twenty Record
34. Towels
35. Transistor Radio
36. Tubular Ladder
37. Vacuum Cleaner
38. Wall Can Opener
39. Washing Machine

Printing C: 9 cards are known, those marked with an * being the common issue

	Left	Right
1. Clothes Dryer	L*	
2, Electric Kettle	L*	
3. Electric Steam Iron		R*
4. Electric Toaster		R*
5. Refrigerator	L*	
6. Tea Caddy		R*
7. Tea Cosy		R*
8. Tea Pot	L*	
9. Three Tea Cloths	L*	

ISSUES OF BROOKE BOND LIEBIG ITALY

The following are all sets of 6 numbered cards size 111 x 70mm inscribed Brooke Bond Liebig Italiana S.p.A. – Milano.and all have Italian text:

	Gli Uccelli Protetti (Protected Birds) issued in 1975 (No series number)
Serie 298	Uniformologia Antica (Old Military Dress) 1st series issued in 1975
Serie 299	Uniformologia Antica (Old Military Dress) 2nd series issued in 1975
Serie 320	Come Siamo Andati Sulla Luna (Journey to the Moon) 1st series issued in 1975
Serie 323	La Nativita (The Nativity) issued in 1971
Serie 324	Storia Della Macchina Per Scrivere (History of the Typewriter) issued in 1972
Serie 325	La Resurrezione (The Resurrection) issued in 1972
Serie 326	Come Siamo Andati Sulla Luna (Journey to the Moon) 2nd series issued in 1975
Serie 327	Le Grandin Sfide (Historical Fights) issued in 1972
Serie 328	Autoritratti Di Grandi Pittori Italiani (Self- Portraits of Famous Artists) issued in 1972
Serie 329	Cosi' Vedono Gli Animali (How Animals See) 1st series issued in 1973
Serie 330	Ludwig Van Beethoven issued in 1973
Serie 331	Cacciatori Di Microbi (The Fight Against Microbes) 1st series issued in 1973
Serie 332	Cosi' Vedono Gli Animali (How Animals See) 2nd series issued in 1973
Serie 333	Storia Del Circo (The Story of the Circus) 1st series issued in 1973
Serie 334	Cacciatori Di Microbi (The Fight Against Microbes) 2nd series issued in 1973
Serie 335	Storia Del Circo (The Story of the Circus) 2nd series issued in 1973
Serie 336	Marina Da Guerra (War at Sea) issued in 1973
Serie 337	Il Regno Animale (Animals) issued in 1973

Note The 5 series listed, issued in 1975, can be collected without Brooke Bond name. These were first published before Brooke Bond was involved with The Liebig company.